$\mathcal{P}$resented to:

_____

$\mathcal{F}$rom:

_____

$\mathcal{D}$ate:

_____

A Simple BOOK OF Prayers

PERSONAL
CONVERSATIONS
WITH GOD

KENNETH & KAREN BOA

HONOR
BOOKS

A Simple Book of Prayers,
Personal Conversations with God
ISBN 1-56292-775-2
Copyright © 2003 by Kenneth and Karen Boa

Published by Honor Books,
An Imprint of Cook Communications Ministries
4050 Lee Vance View
Colorado Springs, CO 89018

Introduction

The Purpose of *A Simple Book of Prayers*

Communicating with God, talking directly and openly with Him just as we would talk with an intimate friend, is one of the great blessings of the spiritual life and the key to a growing relationship with the personal God of Heaven and earth.

Most of us want to pray more than we do, but often we find our prayers unsatisfying and sporadic. It is easy to slip into the extremes of all form and no freedom or all freedom and no form. The first extreme leads to a rote or impersonal approach to prayer, while the second produces an unbalanced and undisciplined prayer life that can degenerate into a series of one "gimme" after another. *A Simple Book of Prayers* makes prayer a more enriching and satisfying experience by providing both form and freedom in prayer. The form is Scripture itself, and the freedom is your own thoughts and prayers in response to the truths of Scripture.

A Simple Book of Prayers combines the Word with prayer and guides you through the process of praying Scripture back to God. You will think God's thoughts after Him and personalize them in your own life. This prayer book will also provide you with a balanced diet of prayer by guiding your mind each day through different kinds of prayer.

Because it is based on Scripture, you can be assured that these prayers will be pleasing to God. This book will encourage you in your walk with God by enriching the quality of your experience of prayer.

The Structure of

A Simple Book of Prayers

Each of these *Simple Prayers* uses the same two-part structure:

The first part provides a weekly cycle of seven kinds of prayers adapted from Scripture: adoration, confession, renewal, petition, intercession, affirmation, and thanksgiving. These prayers are preceded by brief statements to help you personalize them.

The second half contains affirmations adapted from Scripture about the person of God and the works of God as well as affirmations about the character we should want to cultivate and affirmations about our relationships with other people.

To create this collection of biblical prayers and affirmations, I consulted several translations as well as the original language of every passage. The result is my own translation, as close to the biblical text as possible while still retaining clarity and readability.

I adapted the passages into a personalized format for use by individuals and groups. A number of the negative statements and evaluations in the Bible are turned into positive statements. In other cases, principles come from the lives of biblical characters.

PUTTING ON A HEART OF LOVE
Adoration

Lord, I give thanks for Your greatness, your goodness, and your love; and I now draw near to enjoy your presence.

The Son of Man will come with the clouds of heaven. In the presence of the Ancient of Days, He will be given dominion and glory and a kingdom so that all peoples, nations, and men of every language will worship Him. His dominion is an everlasting dominion that will not pass away, and His kingdom is one that will never be destroyed.

DANIEL 7:13-14

Jesus is my Lord and my God.

JOHN 20:28

TAKE A MOMENT TO CONSIDER GOD'S AWESOME MAJESTY, AND THANK HIM THAT HE LOVES YOU AND WANTS AN INTIMATE RELATIONSHIP WITH YOU.

As one who has been chosen of God, holy and beloved, I will put on a heart of compassion, kindness, humility, gentleness, and patience, bearing with others and forgiving others even as the Lord forgave me; and above all these things, I will put on love, which is the bond of perfection.

COLOSSIANS 3:12-14

Lord, I thank You for the universal dominion of Jesus Christ and for the hope of His glorious coming. I thank You for the ministry of Your Holy Spirit, and I ask that I would be compassionate and forgiving toward others.

9

DWELLING ON GOD'S HILL
Confession

I am grateful to You, O God, for the blessing of your forgiveness. I thank You that in Christ You set me free from the guilt of the past and give me hope for the future.

Who may ascend the hill of the Lord?
Who may stand in His holy place?
He who has clean hands and a pure heart,
Who has not lifted up his soul to an idol
Or sworn by what is false.

PSALM 24:3-4

TAKE A MOMENT TO ASK THE SPIRIT TO SEARCH YOUR HEART AND REVEAL ANY AREAS OF UNCONFESSED SIN. ACKNOWLEDGE THESE TO THE LORD, AND THANK HIM FOR HIS FORGIVENESS.

The Lord Jesus Christ received honor and glory from God the Father when the voice came to Him from the Majestic Glory, who said, "This is My beloved Son, with whom I am well pleased."

2 PETER 1:17

In Your unfailing love You have led the people You have redeemed. In Your strength You have guided them to Your holy dwelling. You brought them in and planted them in the mountain of Your inheritance.

EXODUS 15:13, 17

Lord, I thank You that You have become my dwelling place, my Redeemer, and my inheritance. I give thanks that Jesus, Your beloved Son, is exalted above all.

Renewal

I praise You, *Lord*, that You are intimately acquainted with my ways and that You always love me and have my best interests at heart.

May the Lord my God be with me . . . ; may You never leave me nor forsake me. Incline my heart to You, to walk in all Your ways and to keep Your commands and Your statutes and Your judgments.

1 KINGS 8:57-58

As one who knows righteousness, who has Your law in my heart, may I not fear the reproach of men or be terrified by their revilings.

ISAIAH 51:7

TAKE A MOMENT TO OFFER THIS DAY TO THE LORD, AND ASK HIM FOR THE GRACE TO GROW IN YOUR KNOWLEDGE AND LOVE FOR HIM.

You, the Lord, alone have declared what is to come from the distant past. There is no God apart from You, a righteous God and a Savior.

ISAIAH 45:21

The Lord is near to all who call upon Him, to all who call upon Him in truth. He fulfills the desire of those who fear Him; He hears their cry and saves them.

PSALM 145:18-19

Lord, I praise You that You alone are the unchanging, ever-present, compassionate God of heaven and earth, and You are in authority over all things. May I call upon You in truth.

RECEIVING WISDOM
Petition

As I approach Your throne of grace today, I am grateful that You care about the things that concern me and that You want me to offer them up to You.

May I be above reproach, . . . temperate, sensible, respectable, hospitable, able to teach, not given to drunkenness, not violent but gentle, not quarrelsome, not a lover of money, one who manages their own family well, and who keeps their children under control with proper respect. Grant me a good reputation with outsiders so that I will not fall into disgrace and the snare of the devil.

1 TIMOTHY 3:2-4,7

TAKE A MOMENT TO SHARE YOUR PERSONAL NEEDS WITH GOD, INCLUDING YOUR PHYSICAL, EMOTIONAL, RELATIONAL, AND SPIRITUAL CONCERNS.

The Lord gives wisdom; from His mouth come knowledge and understanding. He stores up sound wisdom for the upright; He is a shield to those who walk in integrity, guarding the paths of justice and protects the way of His saints. Then I will understand righteousness and justice and honesty—every good path.

PROVERBS 2:6-9

Lord, I praise Your majesty and that You reached down in love to save us. I thank You that Your nearness is my good, and I ask that I would receive Your wisdom and reverence You above all else.

PLEASING OUR NEIGHBOR
Intercession

Lord, You have invited me to pray for the needs of others; and since You desire what is best for them, I take this opportunity to bring these requests to You.

Blessed are those whose strength is in You,
Who have set their hearts on pilgrimage.

PSALM 84:5

O Lord, be gracious to us; we have hoped in You.
Be our strength every morning,
Our salvation in time of distress.

ISAIAH 33:2

TAKE A MOMENT TO LIFT UP THE NEEDS OF YOUR FAMILY AND FRIENDS, AND TO OFFER UP ANY OTHER BURDENS FOR OTHERS THAT THE LORD BRINGS TO MIND.

We who are strong ought to bear the weaknesses of those who are not strong, and not to please ourselves. Each of us should please our neighbor for their good, to build them up.

ROMANS 15:1-2

No one should seek their own good, but the good of others.

1 CORINTHIANS 10:24

*L*ord, I praise You for Your power and might and for Your lovingkindness. I thank You for being my portion, and I ask that I would be mindful of the needs of others.

GUARDING MY HEART
Affirmation

God, I want Your Word to be deeply implanted in me so that I not only know the truth but also express it in the way I live.

I will both lie down in peace and sleep;
For You alone, O Lord, make me dwell in safety.

PSALM 4:8

I have set the Lord always before me;
Because He is at my right hand, I will not be shaken.
Therefore my heart is glad, and my glory rejoices;
My body also will rest in hope.
You will make known to me the path of life;
In Your presence is fullness of joy;
In Your right hand are pleasures forever.

PSALM 16:8-9, 11

TAKE A MOMENT TO AFFIRM THE TRUTH OF THESE WORDS FROM SCRIPTURE, AND ASK GOD TO MAKE THEM A GROWING REALITY IN YOUR LIFE.

I will guard my heart with all diligence,
for out of it flow the issues of life.

PROVERBS 4:23

The fear of the Lord is the beginning of wisdom,
and the knowledge of the Holy One is understanding.

PROVERBS 9:10

$\mathcal{L}ord$, I praise You for Your surpassing lofti-
ness and for Your dominion over the cosmos.
I thank You for loving me in Christ Jesus.
May I guard my heart and know You better.

Thanksgiving

O Lord, I am deeply grateful for Your wonderful acts, for Your abundant promises, and for the gift of my relationship with You through the merits of Christ.

I will sing to the Lord and give praise to the Lord,
For He has rescued the life of the needy
From the hands of evildoers.

JEREMIAH 20:13

The Lord is good,
A refuge in times of trouble;
He knows those who trust in Him.

NAHUM 1:7

TAKE A MOMENT TO EXPRESS YOUR GRATITUDE FOR THE MANY BLESSINGS THAT YOU HAVE RECEIVED FROM THE LORD.

I will obey those who are in authority over me with fear and trembling and with sincerity of heart, as to Christ; not with external service as a pleaser of men but as a slave of Christ, doing the will of God from my heart. With goodwill, I will serve as to the Lord and not to men, knowing that I will receive back from the Lord whatever good I do.

EPHESIANS 6:5-8

$\mathcal{L}$ord, I praise You for the glory of the incarnate Word and for Your incomparable grandeur. I thank You for the transforming power of Your truth. May I order my steps in humility and in gentleness.

ACQUIRING THE KNOWLEDGE OF GOD

Adoration

Lord, I give thanks for Your greatness, your goodness, and your love; and I now draw near to enjoy your presence.

Where were you when I laid the foundations of the earth?
Tell Me, if you have understanding.
Who determined its measurements? Surely you know!
Or who stretched the line across it?
On what were its bases sunk,
Or who laid its cornerstone,
When the morning stars sang together
And all the sons of God shouted for joy?

JOB 38:4-7

You revealed Yourself to Moses as "I AM WHO I AM."

EXODUS 3:14

TAKE A MOMENT TO CONSIDER GOD'S AWESOME MAJESTY, AND THANK HIM THAT HE LOVES YOU AND WANTS AN INTIMATE RELATIONSHIP WITH YOU.

The heart of the prudent acquires knowledge,
and the ear of the wise seeks knowledge.

PROVERBS 18:15

He who heeds the word prospers,
and blessed is he who trusts in the Lord.

PROVERBS 16:20

Lord, I thank You that You know me, and I pray that I would never be ashamed of my relationship with Jesus Christ. I thank You for being my help and my shield. I ask that I would be prudent enough to acquire knowledge and to heed Your words.

ABIDING IN GOD'S FORGIVENESS
Confession

I am grateful to You, O God, for the blessing of your forgiveness. I thank You that in Christ You set me free from the guilt of the past and give me hope for the future.

> *You have been just in all that has happened to me;*
> *You have acted faithfully, while I did wrong.*
>
> NEHEMIAH 9:33

> *"In repentance and rest is your salvation;*
> *In quietness and trust is your strength."*
>
> ISAIAH 30:15

TAKE A MOMENT TO ASK THE SPIRIT TO SEARCH YOUR HEART AND REVEAL ANY AREAS OF UNCONFESSED SIN. ACKNOWLEDGE THESE TO THE LORD, AND THANK HIM FOR HIS FORGIVENESS.

You are the living God, and there is no god besides You. You put to death and You bring to life, You have wounded and You will heal, and no one can deliver from Your hand.

DEUTERONOMY 32:39

Who is a God like You, who pardons? . . . You do not stay angry forever but delight to show mercy. You will have compassion on Your people; You will tread their iniquities underfoot and hurl all their sins into the depths of the sea.

MICAH 7:18-19

Lord, I thank You for Your great gift of compassion, pardon, and forgiveness, and for Your power and abiding presence in my life. There is no deliverer besides You.

OBEYING THE GOLDEN RULE
Renewal

I praise You, *Lord*, that You are intimately acquainted with my ways and that You always love me and have my best interests at heart.

If I abide in You, and Your words abide in me,
I can ask whatever I wish, and it will be done for me.
As I ask in Your name,
I will receive, that my joy may be full.

JOHN 15:7, 16:24

As I walk in the Spirit, I will not fulfill the desires of the flesh. For the flesh desires what is contrary to the Spirit, and the Spirit what is contrary to the flesh; for they oppose each other so that I may not do the things that I wish.

GALATIANS 5:16-17

TAKE A MOMENT TO OFFER THIS DAY TO THE LORD, AND ASK HIM FOR THE GRACE TO GROW IN YOUR KNOWLEDGE AND LOVE FOR HIM.

*I will not take vengeance
or bear a grudge against others,
but I will love my neighbor as myself.*

LEVITICUS 19:18

Whatever I want others to do to me, I will also do to them.

MATTHEW 7:12

Lord, I thank You for making all things and for understanding the hearts of all. I ask that I would be glad in You and that I would serve others in the way I wish them to treat me.

RUNNING WITH ENDURANCE
Petition

As I approach Your throne of grace today, I am grateful that You care about the things that concern me and that You want me to offer them up to You.

May I lay aside every impediment and the sin that so easily entangles, and run with endurance the race that is set before me, fixing my eyes on Jesus, the author and perfecter of my faith, who for the joy set before Him endured the cross, despising the shame, and sat down at the right hand of the throne of God. May I consider Him who endured such hostility from sinners so that I will not grow weary and lose heart.

HEBREWS 12:1-3

TAKE A MOMENT TO SHARE YOUR PERSONAL NEEDS WITH GOD, INCLUDING YOUR PHYSICAL, EMOTIONAL, RELATIONAL, AND SPIRITUAL CONCERNS.

*I will not set my heart on evil things, or be an idolater,
or commit sexual immorality.*

1 Corinthians 10:6-8

*I will consider the members of my earthly body
as dead to immorality, impurity, passion, evil desires,
and greed, which is idolatry.*

Colossians 3:5

Lord, I thank You for Your lovingkindness
and truth and for Christ's willingness to
humble Himself on behalf of others. I thank
You for seating me at Your right hand in
Christ, and I ask that I would not set my
heart on sinful desires.

GROWING IN CHRIST'S BODY

Intercession

Lord, You have invited me to pray for the needs of others; and since You desire what is best for them, I take this opportunity to bring these requests to You.

> *Restore us again, O God of our salvation,*
> *And put away Your anger toward us. . . .*
> *Will You not revive us again,*
> *That Your people may rejoice in You?*
> *Show us Your lovingkindness, O Lord,*
> *And grant us Your salvation.*
>
> PSALM 85:4, 6-7

TAKE A MOMENT TO LIFT UP THE NEEDS OF YOUR FAMILY AND FRIENDS, AND TO OFFER UP ANY OTHER BURDENS FOR OTHERS THAT THE LORD BRINGS TO MIND.

I have been born again . . . through the living and abiding word of God. Therefore, I will put away all malice and all guile and hypocrisy and envy and all slander.

1 PETER 1:23, 2:1

From Christ the whole body is being joined and held together by every supporting ligament, according to the effective working of each individual part, causing the growth of the body for the edifying of itself in love.

EPHESIANS 4:16

$\mathcal{L}ord$, I thank You that Your ways are righteous and true. You will make all things new. I thank You for reviving me and delivering me in my troubles. May I put away malice and build up others.

APPLYING GOD'S WORD
Affirmation

God, I want Your Word to be deeply implanted in me so that I not only know the truth but also express it in the way I live.

Be exalted, O Lord, in Your strength;
We will sing and praise Your power.

PSALM 21:13

Save Your people and bless Your inheritance;
Be their shepherd and carry them forever.

PSALM 28:9

TAKE A MOMENT TO AFFIRM THE TRUTH OF THESE WORDS FROM SCRIPTURE, AND ASK GOD TO MAKE THEM A GROWING REALITY IN YOUR LIFE.

I will not wear myself out to get rich; I will have the understanding to cease. I will not set my desire on what flies away, for wealth surely sprouts wings and flies into the heavens like an eagle.

PROVERBS 23:4-5

He who oppresses the poor reproaches their Maker, but whoever is kind to the needy honors Him.

PROVERBS 14:31

Lord, I praise You for Your glory and faithfulness and thank You for Christ's body and blood. I thank You that You want me to apply Your word in my life. Please keep me from greed and give me a generous heart.

BEARING THE FRUIT OF
Thanksgiving

RIGHTEOUSNESS

O Lord, I am deeply grateful for Your wonderful acts, for Your abundant promises, and for the gift of my relationship with You through the merits of Christ.

Surely the Lord's hand is not too short to save, nor His ear too dull to hear. But our iniquities have separated us from our God; our sins have hidden His face from us so that He will not hear. Yet the Lord saw that there was no one to intervene; So His own arm worked salvation for Him.

ISAIAH 59:1-2, 16

TAKE A MOMENT TO EXPRESS YOUR GRATITUDE FOR THE MANY BLESSINGS THAT YOU HAVE RECEIVED FROM THE LORD.

"My son, do not despise the Lord's discipline,
nor lose heart when you are rebuked by Him,
for whom the Lord loves He disciplines."

HEBREWS 12:5-6

God disciplines us for our good, that we may share in His holiness. No discipline seems pleasant at the time, but painful; later on, however, it produces the peaceable fruit of righteousness for those who have been trained by it.

HEBREWS 12:10-11

Lord, I prasie You for Your faithfulness and thank You for the powerful ministry of Jesus. I thank You for making me alive to You. May I respond well to Your discipline and bear the peaceable fruit of righteousness.

RESTING IN THE SHADOW OF THE ALMIGHTY
Adoration

Lord, I give thanks for Your greatness,
your goodness, and your love; and I now
draw near to enjoy your presence.

> *How great are Your works, O Lord!*
> *Your thoughts are very deep.*
> *The senseless man does not know;*
> *Fools do not understand.*
> *But You, O Lord, are exalted forever.*
>
> PSALM 92:5-6, 8
>
> *You are the Lord, that is Your name.*
> *You will not give Your glory to another,*
> *Or Your praise to idols.*
>
> ISAIAH 42:8

TAKE A MOMENT TO CONSIDER GOD'S
AWESOME MAJESTY, AND THANK HIM THAT
HE LOVES YOU AND WANTS AN INTIMATE
RELATIONSHIP WITH YOU.

He who dwells in the shelter of the Most High
will rest in the shadow of the Almighty.
I will say of the Lord, "He is my refuge and my fortress."

PSALM 91:1-2

Christ has appeared once for all at the end of the ages to do away with sin by the sacrifice of Himself. And as it is appointed for man to die once and, after that to face judgment, so Christ was offered once to bear the sins of many.

HEBREWS 9:26-28

*L*ord, I praise You for Your great lovingkindness, Your righteousness, Your faithfulness, and Your justice. I give thanks for the newness of life that has been made available through the death and resurrection of Christ Jesus. May I rest in the shelter of Your salvation.

LOVING OTHERS
Confession

I am grateful to You, *O God*, for the blessing of your forgiveness. I thank You that in Christ You set me free from the guilt of the past and give me hope for the future.

When I sin against the Lord,
I may be sure that my sin will find me out.

NUMBERS 32:23

Come, let us return to the Lord.
For He has torn us, but He will heal us;
He has injured us but He will bind up our wounds.

HOSEA 6:1

TAKE A MOMENT TO ASK THE SPIRIT TO SEARCH YOUR HEART AND REVEAL ANY AREAS OF UNCONFESSED SIN. ACKNOW-LEDGE THESE TO THE LORD, AND THANK HIM FOR HIS FORGIVENESS.

I do not dare to classify or compare myself with other people, for it is unwise to measure or compare myself with others. I will not boast beyond proper limits but within the sphere of the gospel of Christ. "Let him who boasts, boast in the Lord."

2 CORINTHIANS 10:12-14, 17

I will not hate my brother in my heart.

LEVITICUS 19:17

Lord, I praise You for Your authority over the nations and for the righteous judgment that You will bring to the world. I thank You that You have placed my life in Christ. I ask that I would love others and boast only in Him.

CLINGING TO HIS HOPE
Renewal

I praise You, *Lord*, that You are intimately acquainted with my ways and that You always love me and have my best interests at heart.

May I not be conformed to the pattern of this world but be transformed by the renewing of my mind, that I may prove that the will of God is good and acceptable and perfect.

ROMANS 12:2

May the eyes of my heart be enlightened, in order that I may know what is the hope of His calling, what are the riches of His glorious inheritance in the saints, and what is the incomparable greatness of His power toward us who believe.

EPHESIANS 1:18-19

TAKE A MOMENT TO OFFER THIS DAY TO THE LORD, AND ASK HIM FOR THE GRACE TO GROW IN YOUR KNOWLEDGE AND LOVE FOR HIM.

I will not seek glory from people.

1 THESSALONIANS 2: 6

*I will work out my salvation with fear and trembling,
for it is God who works in me to will and to act
according to His good purpose.*

PHILIPPIANS 2:12-13

*L*ord, I praise You for Your compassion and graciousness, and for the authority of the resurrected Christ. I thank You for the gift of the new birth. May I seek to please You and depend upon You.

DEVOTING MYSELF TO HIM
Petition

As I approach Your throne of grace today, I am grateful that You care about the things that concern me and that You want me to offer them up to You.

> *Do not let my heart envy sinners,*
> *But let me live only in the fear of the Lord.*
> *For surely there is a future,*
> *And my hope will not be cut off.*
>
> PROVERBS 23:17-18

TAKE A MOMENT TO SHARE YOUR PERSONAL NEEDS WITH GOD, INCLUDING YOUR PHYSICAL, EMOTIONAL, RELATIONAL, AND SPIRITUAL CONCERNS.

The Lord is my portion; I have promised to keep
Your words. I considered my ways
and turned my steps to Your testimonies.

PSALM 119:57, 59

I will devote myself to prayer,
being watchful in it with thanksgiving.

COLOSSIANS 4:2

Lord, I praise You for Your goodness and
unfailing love, and thank You for Your assurance that Christ will return and bring justice
to the earth. Thank You for being my strong
fortress. May I be devoted to knowing and
following You.

DELIGHTING IN THE WORD
Intercession

Lord, You have invited me to pray for the needs of others; and since You desire what is best for them, I take this opportunity to bring these requests to You.

All of us have become like one who is unclean,
And all our righteous acts are like filthy rags. . . .
But now, O Lord, You are our Father.
We are the clay; You are the potter;
We are all the work of Your hand.

ISAIAH 64:6, 8

TAKE A MOMENT TO LIFT UP THE NEEDS OF YOUR FAMILY AND FRIENDS, AND TO OFFER UP ANY OTHER BURDENS FOR OTHERS THAT THE LORD BRINGS TO MIND.

Blessed is the man who does not walk in the counsel of the wicked or stand in the way of sinners or sit in the seat of scorners. But his delight is in the law of the Lord, and in His law he meditates day and night. . . . and whatever he does will prosper.

PSALM 1:1-3

I will contribute to the needs of the saints and practice hospitality.

ROMANS 12:13

*L*ord, I praise You that Your judgments are true and righteous. You give life to all things. I thank You for the hope of the resurrection. May I delight in Your word and serve the needs of others.

45

PROCLAIMING HIS SALVATION

Affirmation

God, I want Your Word to be deeply implanted in me so that I not only know the truth but also express it in the way I live.

> *My soul waits in hope for the Lord;*
> *He is my help and my shield.*
> *My heart rejoices in Him,*
> *Because I trust in His holy name.*
> *Let Your unfailing love be upon us, O Lord,*
> *Even as we put our hope in You.*
>
> PSALM 33:20-22

TAKE A MOMENT TO AFFIRM THE TRUTH OF THESE WORDS FROM SCRIPTURE, AND ASK GOD TO MAKE THEM A GROWING REALITY IN YOUR LIFE.

I want to be an example for other believers in speech, in behavior, in love, in faith, and in purity.

1 TIMOTHY 4:12

How beautiful on the mountains are the feet of those who bring good news, who proclaim peace, who bring good tidings, who proclaim salvation.

ISAIAH 52:7, NAHUM 1:15

*L*ord, I praise You for the light of Christ and that all things will become visible in Him. You are my life and the length of my days, and I ask that I would be an example for others. May I proclaim Your salvation.

PRAYING FOR THE HARVEST
Thanksgiving

O Lord, I am deeply grateful for Your wonderful acts, for Your abundant promises, and for the gift of my relationship with You through the merits of Christ.

> *I will give thanks to the Lord, call upon His name,*
> *And make known to others what He has done.*
>
> 1 CHRONICLES 16:8

> *I know that the Lord has set apart the godly for Himself;*
> *The Lord hears when I call to Him.*
>
> PSALM 4:3

TAKE A MOMENT TO EXPRESS YOUR GRATI-TUDE FOR THE MANY BLESSINGS THAT YOU HAVE RECEIVED FROM THE LORD.

The harvest is plentiful, but the workers are few. Therefore, I will pray that the Lord of the harvest will send out workers into His harvest.

MATTHEW 9:37-38; LUKE 10:2

Behold, I say to you, lift up your eyes and look at the fields, for they are white for harvest. Even now the reaper draws his wages, and gathers fruit for eternal life, that he who sows and he who reaps may rejoice together.

JOHN 4:35-36

Lord, I praise You that You reign over all things and thank You that Christ is preparing us for union with Him. I thank You that You give grace and glory, and I ask that I would be privileged to participate in Your harvest.

ENJOYING GOD'S LOVE
Adoration

Lord, I give thanks for Your greatness,
your goodness, and your love; and I now
draw near to enjoy your presence.

*Great is the Lord and most worthy of praise; His greatness
is unsearchable.*

PSALM 145:3

The Almighty is beyond our reach;
He is exalted in power
And in His justice and great righteousness,
He does not oppress.

JOB 37:23

TAKE A MOMENT TO CONSIDER GOD'S
AWESOME MAJESTY, AND THANK HIM THAT
HE LOVES YOU AND WANTS AN INTIMATE
RELATIONSHIP WITH YOU.

*The Lord upholds all who fall
And lifts up all who are bowed down.
You open Your hand
And satisfy the desire of every living thing.*

PSALM 145:14, 16

Jesus Christ is the faithful witness, the firstborn from the dead, and the ruler of the kings of the earth. To Him who loves us and has freed us from our sins by His blood and has made us to be a kingdom and priests to serve His God and Father; to Him be glory and power for ever and ever.

REVELATION 1:5-6

Lord, I praise You for Your precious and boundless thoughts. Thank You for Jesus who has freed me from the bondage of sin and called me to serve You in newness of life.

RELYING ON HIS PROMISES
Confession

I am grateful to You, *O God*, for the blessing of your forgiveness. I thank You that in Christ You set me free from the guilt of the past and give me hope for the future.

> "For a brief moment I forsook you,
> But with great compassion I will gather you."
>
> ISAIAH 54:7

TAKE A MOMENT TO ASK THE SPIRIT TO SEARCH YOUR HEART AND REVEAL ANY AREAS OF UNCONFESSED SIN. ACKNOWLEDGE THESE TO THE LORD, AND THANK HIM FOR HIS FORGIVENESS.

God is not a man, that He should lie, nor a son of man, that He should change his mind. Has He spoken and not done it? Has He promised and not fulfilled it?

NUMBERS 23:19

The foolishness of God is wiser than men, and the weakness of God is stronger than men. But God chose the foolish things of the world to shame the wise, and God chose the weak things of the world to shame the strong. . . . so that no one may boast before Him.

1 CORINTHIANS 1:25, 27-29

Lord, I praise You that Your promises are always true. You are my unfailing source of hope and trust in an uncertain world. I am grateful that You have chosen me for Yourself.

PRAYING FOR THE LOST
Renewal

I praise You, $\mathcal{L}$*ord, that You are intimately acquainted with my ways and that You always love me and have my best interests at heart.*

> *Like Job, may I be blameless and upright,*
> *fearing God and shunning evil.*
>
> JOB 1:1

May I be careful to lead a blameless life. May I walk in the integrity of my heart in the midst of my house. May I set no wicked thing before my eyes.

PSALM 101:2-3

TAKE A MOMENT TO OFFER THIS DAY TO THE LORD, AND ASK HIM FOR THE GRACE TO GROW IN YOUR KNOWLEDGE AND LOVE FOR HIM.

I should offer petitions, prayers, intercessions, and thanksgivings on behalf of all men. . . . This is good and acceptable in the sight of God our Savior, who desires all men to be saved and to come to the knowledge of the truth.

1 TIMOTHY 2:1-4

I pray that God may open to me a door for the word so that I may speak the mystery of Christ and proclaim it clearly, as I ought to speak.

COLOSSIANS 4:3-4

Lord, I praise You for Your rule over all things and for the earthly ministry of Jesus. I thank You for the power of Your word, and I ask that I would intercede in prayer for others.

MEASURING OUT COMPASSION
Petition

As I approach Your throne of grace today, I am grateful that You care about the things that concern me and that You want me to offer them up to You.

> *Out of the depths I have called to You, O Lord.*
> *O Lord, hear my voice,*
> *And let Your ears be attentive*
> *To the voice of my supplications.*

PSALM 130:1-2

TAKE A MOMENT TO SHARE YOUR PERSONAL NEEDS WITH GOD, INCLUDING YOUR PHYSICAL, EMOTIONAL, RELATIONAL, AND SPIRITUAL CONCERNS.

*He who heeds instruction is on the path of life,
but he who refuses correction goes astray.*

PROVERBS 10:17

I will not judge so that I will not be judged. For in the same way I judge others, I will be judged; and with the measure I use, it will be measured to me.

MATTHEW 7:1-2

Lord, I thank You that You know me intimately and that Jesus serves people with love and compassion. I thank You that You call me to bear much fruit. Please give me a humble heart that responds to Your rebuke and keep me from judging others.

PRAISING GOD'S WORK
Intercession

Lord, You have invited me to pray for the needs of others; and since You desire what is best for them, I take this opportunity to bring these requests to You.

If two of you agree on earth about anything they may ask, it will be done for them by My Father in heaven. Where two or three come together in My name, I am there in their midst.

MATTHEW 18:19-20

May we be devoted to one another in brotherly love, honoring one another above ourselves.

ROMANS 12:10

TAKE A MOMENT TO LIFT UP THE NEEDS OF YOUR FAMILY AND FRIENDS, AND TO OFFER UP ANY OTHER BURDENS FOR OTHERS THAT THE LORD BRINGS TO MIND.

I will regard the Lord of hosts as holy;
He shall be my fear,
And He shall be my dread.

ISAIAH 8:13

What is man that You are mindful of him, and the son of man that You care for him? You made him a little lower than the heavenly beings and crowned him with glory and honor.

PSALM 8:4-5

Lord, I praise You for the magnificent work of Your elegant, intricate, and beautiful created order. You are exalted in power, yet You are mindful of Your people. May I hold you in highest honor and holy respect.

BEING STILL AND BEING UNIFIED
Affirmation

God, I want Your Word to be deeply implanted in me so that I not only know the truth but also express it in the way I live.

Blessed be the Lord, the God of Israel,
From everlasting to everlasting.
Amen and Amen.

PSALM 41:13

I will be still and know that You are God;
You will be exalted among the nations,
You will be exalted in the earth.

PSALM 46:10

TAKE A MOMENT TO AFFIRM THE TRUTH OF THESE WORDS FROM SCRIPTURE, AND ASK GOD TO MAKE THEM A GROWING REALITY IN YOUR LIFE.

The integrity of the upright guides them.

PROVERBS 11:3

The Lord Jesus prayed these words for the unity of all who would believe in Him: "I ask that all of them may be one, Father, just as You are in Me and I am in You, that they also may be in Us . . . that the world may know that You have sent Me and have loved them, even as You have loved Me."

JOHN 17:21-23

*L*ord, I praise You for the perfection of Your way and for the blood of Christ that makes me righteous in Your sight. You have blessed me with every spiritual blessing. May I live in integrity and seek unity with other believers.

FULFILLING THE LAW OF LOVE
Thanksgiving

O Lord, I am deeply grateful for Your wonderful acts, for Your abundant promises, and for the gift of my relationship with You through the merits of Christ.

I will give thanks to the Lord according to His righteousness.

PSALM 7:17

The Lord is my light and my salvation;
Whom shall I fear?
The Lord is the strength of my life;
Of whom shall I be afraid?

PSALM 27:1

TAKE A MOMENT TO EXPRESS YOUR GRATITUDE FOR THE MANY BLESSINGS THAT YOU HAVE RECEIVED FROM THE LORD.

I am not trying to win the approval of men, but of God. If I were still trying to please men, I would not be a servant of Christ.

GALATIANS 1:10

I will owe nothing to anyone except to love them, for he who loves his neighbor has fulfilled the law. . . . If there is any other commandment, it is summed up in this saying: "You shall love your neighbor as yourself." Love does no harm to a neighbor; therefore love is the fulfillment of the law.

ROMANS 13:8-10

Lord, I thank You for reviving the spirit of the lowly and for raising Your Son from the dead. I thank You for bearing my burdens, and I ask that I would seek to serve Christ by loving others.

ACKNOWLEDGING HIS GREATNESS
Adoration

Lord, I give thanks for Your greatness,
your goodness, and your love; and I now
draw near to enjoy your presence.

Who has measured the waters in the hollow of His hand,
Or marked off the heavens with the breadth of his hand?
Who has calculated the dust of the earth in a measure,
Or weighed the mountains in the balance
And the hills in scales?

ISAIAH 40:12

You are the Lord, and there is no other;
Apart from You there is no God.

ISAIAH 45:5-6

TAKE A MOMENT TO CONSIDER GOD'S
AWESOME MAJESTY, AND THANK HIM THAT
HE LOVES YOU AND WANTS AN INTIMATE
RELATIONSHIP WITH YOU.

I will not slander other believers. . . . There is only one Lawgiver and Judge, the One who is able to save and to destroy. Who am I to judge my neighbor?

JAMES 4:11-12

The one who loves his brother abides in the light, and there is no cause for stumbling in him. But the one who hates his brother is in the darkness and walks in the darkness and does not know where he is going because the darkness has blinded his eyes.

1 JOHN 2:10-11

$\mathcal{L}$*ord*, I praise You for the living power of Your word and for the abundance of Your grace. I thank You for creating and loving me. May I not slander others, but love them.

REMEMBERING HIS GOODNESS
Confession

I am grateful to You, O God, for the blessing of your forgiveness. I thank You that in Christ You set me free from the guilt of the past and give me hope for the future.

When my soul was fainting away,
I remembered the Lord,
And my prayer went up to You, to Your holy temple.
I will fulfill what I have vowed.
Salvation is from the Lord.

JONAH 2:7,9

TAKE A MOMENT TO ASK THE SPIRIT TO SEARCH YOUR HEART AND REVEAL ANY AREAS OF UNCONFESSED SIN. ACKNOWLEDGE THESE TO THE LORD, AND THANK HIM FOR HIS FORGIVENESS.

When I am blessed with abundance, I will beware lest my heart becomes proud, and I forget the Lord my God who provided all good things, thinking that it was my power and the strength of my hand that brought this wealth.

DEUTERONOMY 8:12-14, 17

All things are for our sakes so that the grace that is reaching more and more people may cause thanksgiving to abound to the glory of God.

2 CORINTHIANS 4:15

Lord, I thank You for Christ and for His sufferings on my behalf. I thank You that I have the power to walk in the Spirit, and I acknowledge You as the source of every good thing. May I be generous to others.

67

Renewal

DOING GOOD DEEDS

I praise You, *Lord*, that You are intimately acquainted with my ways and that You always love me and have my best interests at heart.

I must let my light shine before men, that they may see my good deeds and praise my Father in heaven.

MATTHEW 5:16

I want to walk in a way that is worthy of the calling with which I was called, with all humility and meekness and patience.

EPHESIANS 4:1-2

TAKE A MOMENT TO OFFER THIS DAY TO THE LORD, AND ASK HIM FOR THE GRACE TO GROW IN YOUR KNOWLEDGE AND LOVE FOR HIM.

I will keep my life free from the love of money . . . for You have said, "I will never leave you, nor will I forsake you."

HEBREWS 13:5

"For I was hungry, and you gave Me something to eat; I was thirsty, and you gave Me something to drink; I was a stranger, and you invited Me in; I was naked, and you clothed Me; I was sick, and you visited Me; I was in prison, and you came to Me."

MATTHEW 25:35-37

$\mathcal{L}$ord, I thank You for wisdom in Christ. I thank You that I will know Jesus fully. May I be content with what I have, and do good deeds toward others.

BOASTING IN THE LORD
Petition

As I approach *Your* throne of grace today, I am grateful that You care about the things that concern me and that You want me to offer them up to You.

> O Lord, hear my prayer;
> Listen to the voice of my supplications.
> In the day of my trouble I will call upon You,
> For You will answer me.
> You are great and do wondrous deeds;
> You alone are God.
>
> PSALM 86:6-7, 10

TAKE A MOMENT TO SHARE YOUR PERSONAL NEEDS WITH GOD, INCLUDING YOUR PHYSICAL, EMOTIONAL, RELATIONAL, AND SPIRITUAL CONCERNS.

I will not boast about tomorrow,
for I do not know what a day may bring forth.

PROVERBS 27:1

Thus says the Lord: "Let not the wise man boast of his wisdom, and let not the strong man boast of his strength, and let not the rich man boast of his riches; but let him who boasts, boast about this: that he understands and knows Me, that I am the Lord, who exercises lovingkindness, justice, and righteousness on earth; for in these I delight," declares the Lord.

JEREMIAH 9:23-24

Lord, I thank You for Your loyal love and truth and for Your great and awesome wonders. I thank You that I have been born of God through faith in Christ Jesus. May I boast only of You.

LOVING OTHERS SINCERELY
Intercession

Lord, You have invited me to pray for the needs of others; and since You desire what is best for them, I take this opportunity to bring these requests to You.

> *Far be it from me*
> *that I should sin against the Lord*
> *by ceasing to pray for others.*
>
> 1 SAMUEL 12:23

Oh, that they would always have such a heart to fear Me and keep all My commandments so that it might be well with them and with their children forever!

DEUTERONOMY 5:29

TAKE A MOMENT TO LIFT UP THE NEEDS OF YOUR FAMILY AND FRIENDS, AND TO OFFER UP ANY OTHER BURDENS FOR OTHERS THAT THE LORD BRINGS TO MIND.

May the Lord make me increase and abound
in my love for believers and for unbelievers.

1 THESSALONIANS 3:12

In obedience to the truth I will purify my soul for a sincere love of the brethren, and I will love others fervently from the heart.

1 PETER 1:22

$\mathcal{L}$*ord*, I thank You for Your righteousness and for Jesus' sufferings on my behalf. I thank You that Your word gives me stability, and I ask that I increase in my love for others.

ORDERING MY STEPS FOR JUSTICE

Affirmation

God, I want Your Word to be deeply implanted in me so that I not only know the truth but also express it in the way I live.

When I remember You on my bed,
I meditate on You through the watches of the night.
Because You have been my help,
I will rejoice in the shadow of Your wings.
My soul clings to You;
Your right hand upholds me.

PSALM 63:6-8

TAKE A MOMENT TO AFFIRM THE TRUTH OF THESE WORDS FROM SCRIPTURE, AND ASK GOD TO MAKE THEM A GROWING REALITY IN YOUR LIFE.

These are the things I shall do: speak the truth to others, judge with truth and justice for peace, not plot evil against my neighbor, and not love a false oath; for all these things the Lord hates.

ZECHARIAH 8:16-17

I will remember those who led me, who spoke the word of God to me. I will consider the outcome of their way of life and imitate their faith.

HEBREWS 13:7

$\mathcal{L}$ord, I thank You that nothing is too difficult for You and that Christ will return to raise us from the dead. I ask that I would abide in Christ, and that I would order my steps in righteousness and service to others.

SEEKING COMPASSION
Thanksgiving

O Lord, I am deeply grateful for Your wonderful acts, for Your abundant promises, and for the gift of my relationship with You through the merits of Christ.

Many, O Lord my God, are the wonders You have done,
And Your thoughts toward us no one can recount to You;
Were I to speak and tell of them, They would be too many
to declare.

PSALM 40:5

I will praise You forever for what You have done;
I will hope in Your name, for it is good.
I will praise You in the presence of Your saints.

PSALM 52:9

TAKE A MOMENT TO EXPRESS YOUR GRATITUDE FOR THE MANY BLESSINGS THAT YOU HAVE RECEIVED FROM THE LORD.

He who covers a transgression seeks love,
but he who repeats a matter separates close friends.

PROVERBS 17:9

I will put away all bitterness and anger and wrath and shouting and slander, along with all malice. And I will be kind and compassionate to others, forgiving them just as God in Christ also forgave me.

EPHESIANS 4:31-32

Lord, I praise You that Your eternal purpose will stand and that You give life to the dead. I thank You for the gift of eternal life in Your Son, and I ask that I would put away bitterness and wrath and show kindness and compassion to others.

LOVING INSTRUCTION
Adoration

Lord, I give thanks for Your greatness, your goodness, and your love; and I now draw near to enjoy your presence.

Great is the Lord and most worthy of praise; He is to be feared above all gods. For all the gods of the nations are idols, but the Lord made the heavens. Splendor and majesty are before Him; strength and beauty are in His sanctuary. I will ascribe to the Lord glory and strength. I will ascribe to the Lord the glory due His name and worship the Lord in the beauty of holiness.

PSALM 96:4-9

Blessed is the man who fears the Lord,
Who finds great delight in His commands.

PSALM 112:1

TAKE A MOMENT TO CONSIDER GOD'S AWESOME MAJESTY, AND THANK HIM THAT HE LOVES YOU AND WANTS AN INTIMATE RELATIONSHIP WITH YOU.

A rebuke goes deeper into a wise person
than a hundred lashes into a fool.

PROVERBS 17:10

Whoever loves instruction loves knowledge,
but the one who hates correction is stupid.

PROVERBS 12:1

*L*ord, I thank You that You know me intimately and still care for me. I thank You for
what You are preparing for those who love
You, and I ask that I would learn from
rebukes and accept correction.

OFFERING THE SACRIFICE OF PRAISE
Confession

I am grateful to You, O God, for the blessing of your forgiveness. I thank You that in Christ You set me free from the guilt of the past and give me hope for the future.

I confess my iniquity;
I am troubled by my sin.
O Lord, do not forsake me;
O my God, be not far from me!
Make haste to help me,
O Lord, my salvation.

PSALM 38:18, 21-22

TAKE A MOMENT TO ASK THE SPIRIT TO SEARCH YOUR HEART AND REVEAL ANY AREAS OF UNCONFESSED SIN. ACKNOW-LEDGE THESE TO THE LORD, AND THANK HIM FOR HIS FORGIVENESS.

The Lord Most High is awesome, the great King over all the earth! God is the King of all the earth, and I will sing His praise.

PSALM 47:2, 7

As living stones, we are being built into a spiritual house to be a holy priesthood, offering spiritual sacrifices acceptable to God through Jesus Christ. We are a chosen people, a royal priesthood, a holy nation, a people for God's own possession.

1 PETER 2:5, 9

Lord, I praise You for Your sovereign rule, and I anticipate the day when all beings acknowledge Your majesty and authority. I thank You that You have called me to know and serve You.

LIVING IN PURITY
Renewal

I praise You, $\mathcal{L}ord$, that You are intimately acquainted with my ways and that You always love me and have my best interests at heart.

> May I fear God and keep His commandments,
> for this applies to every person.
>
> <small>ECCLESIASTES 12:13</small>

Give me understanding, and I will keep Your law And observe it with all my heart. Make me walk in the path of Your commands, For there I find delight. Incline my heart to Your testimonies And not to selfish gain. Turn my eyes away from worthless things, And revive me in Your way.

<small>PSALM 119:34-37</small>

Take a moment to offer this day to the Lord, and ask Him for the grace to grow in your knowledge and love for Him.

*I desire to have a clear conscience
and to live honorably in all things.*

HEBREWS 13:18

*As an alien and a stranger in the world,
I will abstain from fleshly lusts,
which war against my soul.*

1 PETER 2:11

*L*ord, I thank You for Your compassion for the afflicted and the poor and the way in which Your Son demonstrated that compassion. I thank You that He is the living bread that came down from heaven, and I ask that I would abstain from those things that are displeasing to You.

KEEPING THE BOND OF PEACE
Petition

As I approach Your throne of grace today, I am grateful that You care about the things that concern me and that You want me to offer them up to You.

May it be unto me as you said to Jacob,
"Behold, I am with you and will watch over you
wherever you go;
I will not leave you
until I have done what I have promised you."

GENESIS 28:15

TAKE A MOMENT TO SHARE YOUR PERSONAL NEEDS WITH GOD, INCLUDING YOUR PHYSICAL, EMOTIONAL, RELATIONAL, AND SPIRITUAL CONCERNS.

We should ask that the name of our Lord Jesus may be glorified in others, and they in Him, according to the grace of our God and the Lord Jesus Christ.

2 Thessalonians 1:12

*We should bear with one another in love
and make every effort to keep the unity of the
Spirit in the bond of peace.*

Ephesians 4:2-3

Lord, I praise You for Your greatness and thank You for the love that You manifested in sending Your only begotten Son into the world. Your lovingkindness is better than life, and may I seek to honor the name of Jesus Christ and show forbearance to others.

LOVING ONE ANOTHER
Intercession

Lord, You have invited me to pray for the needs of others; and since You desire what is best for them, I take this opportunity to bring these requests to You.

You have given us a new commandment to love one another even as You have loved us; so we must love one another. By this all men will know that we are Your disciples.

JOHN 13:34-35

This is Your commandment, that we love one another as You have loved us.

JOHN 15:12

TAKE A MOMENT TO LIFT UP THE NEEDS OF YOUR FAMILY AND FRIENDS, AND TO OFFER UP ANY OTHER BURDENS FOR OTHERS THAT THE LORD BRINGS TO MIND.

There are six things the Lord hates, seven that are detestable to Him: haughty eyes, a lying tongue, hands that shed innocent blood, a heart that devises wicked plans, feet that run swiftly to evil, a false witness who breathes lies, and one who causes strife among brothers.

PROVERBS 6:16-19

I will be careful that no one entices me by riches.

JOB 36:18

Lord, I praise You for the glory and majesty of Jesus Christ and thank You for the gift of forgiveness through His death and resurrection. You are my strength and my shield. May I put aside those things that are displeasing to You.

CARING FOR OTHERS
Affirmation

God, I want Your Word to be deeply
implanted in me so that I not only know the
truth but also express it in the way I live.

*I will not fear, for You are with me; I will not be dismayed,
for You are my God. You will strengthen me and help me;
You will uphold me with Your righteous right hand. For You
are the Lord my God, who takes hold of my right hand and
says to me, "Do not fear; I will help you."*

ISAIAH 41:10, 13

TAKE A MOMENT TO AFFIRM THE TRUTH OF
THESE WORDS FROM SCRIPTURE, AND ASK
GOD TO MAKE THEM A GROWING REALITY
IN YOUR LIFE.

Woe to those who call evil good and good evil,
who put darkness for light and light for darkness,
who put bitter for sweet and sweet for bitter.

ISAIAH 5:20

We must take heed to ourselves and to all the flock
of which the Holy Spirit has made us overseers
to shepherd the church of God.

ACTS 20:28

Lord, I praise You. You are the God of all mankind. Everyone who believes in Christ will receive forgiveness of sins. I thank You for the richness of Your mercy. May I take heed to myself and guide others into the truth of Your Word.

REJOICING IN HIS LIFE
Thanksgiving

O Lord, I am deeply grateful for Your wonderful acts, for Your abundant promises, and for the gift of my relationship with You through the merits of Christ.

I will praise You, O Lord my God, with all my heart,
And I will glorify Your name forever.
For great is Your love toward me,
And You have delivered my soul from the depths of the grave.

PSALM 86:12-13

Rejoice in the Lord, you who are righteous,
And give thanks at the remembrance of His holy name.

PSALM 97:12

TAKE A MOMENT TO EXPRESS YOUR GRATITUDE FOR THE MANY BLESSINGS THAT YOU HAVE RECEIVED FROM THE LORD.

Where can I go from Your Spirit? Or where can I flee from Your presence? . . . If I take the wings of the dawn, if I dwell in the furthest part of the sea, even there Your hand will lead me; Your right hand will lay hold of me.

PSALM 139:7-10

*For God did not send His Son into the world
to condemn the world,
but to save the world through Him.*

JOHN 3:17

Lord, I thank You that You are ever-present in my life. Nothing can separate me from Your love. I thank You for the highest expression of this love: the gift of eternal life through Jesus Christ.

COVERING OTHERS' SIN

Adoration

Lord, I give thanks for Your greatness, your goodness, and your love; and I now draw near to enjoy your presence.

May I fear You, the Lord my God; may I serve You, hold fast to You, and take my oaths in Your name. For You are my praise, and You are my God, who performed for me these great and awesome wonders which I have seen with my own eyes.

Deuteronomy 10:20-21

You are the great, the mighty, and the awesome God, who keeps His covenant of lovingkindness.

Nehemiah 9:32

TAKE A MOMENT TO CONSIDER GOD'S AWESOME MAJESTY, AND THANK HIM THAT HE LOVES YOU AND WANTS AN INTIMATE RELATIONSHIP WITH YOU.

*Above all, I will have a fervent love for others
because love covers a multitude of sins.*

1 PETER 4:8

*If I forgive men for their transgressions,
my heavenly Father will also forgive me.*

MATTHEW 6:14

*L*ord, I thank You for Your eternal plan
and for creating the heavens and the earth.
I thank You that the Holy Spirit lives in me,
and I ask that I would love others and
forgive them just as I have been forgiven.

ACCEPTING OTHERS
Confession

> I am grateful to You, *O God,* for the
> blessing of your forgiveness. I thank You that
> in Christ You set me free from the guilt of
> the past and give me hope for the future.

> *From within, out of the heart of men, proceed evil
> thoughts, sexual immorality, thefts, murders, adulteries,
> greed, wickedness, deceit, lewdness, envy, slander,
> arrogance, and folly. All these evil things come from within
> and defile a man.*

> MARK 7:21-23

TAKE A MOMENT TO ASK THE SPIRIT TO
SEARCH YOUR HEART AND REVEAL ANY
AREAS OF UNCONFESSED SIN. ACKNOW-
LEDGE THESE TO THE LORD, AND THANK
HIM FOR HIS FORGIVENESS.

*I will rejoice with those who rejoice
and weep with those who weep.*

ROMANS 12:15

*I will accept others, just as Christ accepted me
to the glory of God.*

ROMANS 15:7

$\mathcal{L}$ord, I praise You for Your glory and strength and for Christ's service to those who did not realize who He was. I thank You that You reward those who are persecuted for Your sake, and I ask that I would show compassion and acceptance to others.

WALKING IN FREEDOM
Renewal

I praise You, $\mathcal{L}$ord, that You are intimately acquainted with my ways and that You always love me and have my best interests at heart.

I will not let sin reign in my mortal body that I should obey its lusts. Nor will I present the members of my body to sin, as instruments of wickedness, but I will present myself to God as one who is alive from the dead.

ROMANS 6:12-13

May I put away all filthiness and the overflow of wickedness; and in meekness accept the word planted in me, which is able to save my soul.

JAMES 1:21

TAKE A MOMENT TO OFFER THIS DAY TO THE LORD, AND ASK HIM FOR THE GRACE TO GROW IN YOUR KNOWLEDGE AND LOVE FOR HIM.

*I shall not covet my neighbor's house,
my neighbor's wife . . .
or anything that belongs to my neighbor.*

EXODUS 20:17; DEUTERONOMY 5:21

*I was called to freedom,
but I will not use my freedom to indulge the flesh,
but through love I will serve others.*

GALATIANS 5:13

Lord, I praise You. You endure forever. I thank You for the Lord Jesus, who came in Your name. I thank You for a future and a hope. May I not be covetous or indulge the flesh, but instead may I serve others in love.

BEING OF ONE MIND
Petition

As I approach Your throne of grace today, I am grateful that You care about the things that concern me and that You want me to offer them up to You.

> *May I be strong and courageous,*
> *being careful to obey Your word;*
> *may I not turn from it to the right or to the left,*
> *that I may act wisely wherever I go.*
>
> JOSHUA 1:7

TAKE A MOMENT TO SHARE YOUR PERSONAL NEEDS WITH GOD, INCLUDING YOUR PHYSICAL, EMOTIONAL, RELATIONAL, AND SPIRITUAL CONCERNS.

May the God who gives endurance and encouragement grant us to be of the same mind toward one another according to Christ Jesus so that with one accord and one mouth we may glorify the God and Father of our Lord Jesus Christ.

ROMANS 15:5-6

There should be no division in the body, but its members should have the same concern for each other. If one member suffers, all the members suffer with it; if one member is honored, all the members rejoice with it.

1 CORINTHIANS 12:25-26

Lord, I praise You for Your wondrous power and for the greatness of Your salvation in Jesus. I thank You for instructing and teaching me in the way I should go. May I be concerned for the welfare and unity of the body of Christ.

GOING ON TO MATURITY
Intercession

Lord, You have invited me to pray for the needs of others; and since You desire what is best for them, I take this opportunity to bring these requests to You.

Many are saying, "Who will show us any good?"
O Lord, lift up the light of Your countenance upon us.

PSALM 4:6

Who is the man who desires life and loves many days that he may see good? Keep your tongue from evil and your lips from speaking guile. Depart from evil and do good; seek peace and pursue it. The eyes of the Lord are on the righteous, and His ears are attentive to their cry.

PSALM 34:12-15

TAKE A MOMENT TO LIFT UP THE NEEDS OF YOUR FAMILY AND FRIENDS, AND TO OFFER UP ANY OTHER BURDENS FOR OTHERS THAT THE LORD BRINGS TO MIND.

*I will not enter the path of the wicked
or walk in the way of evil men.*

PROVERBS 4:14

*Anyone who partakes only of milk is not
accustomed to the word of righteousness,
for he is an infant.*

HEBREWS 5:13

Lord, Jesus is my Lord and my God and
I am not ashamed of Him. Thank You that
Christ now lives in me. May I go on to
maturity in Him.

ABOUNDING IN GRACE
Affirmation

God, I want Your Word to be deeply implanted in me so that I not only know the truth but also express it in the way I live.

Father in heaven,
Hallowed be Your name.
Your kingdom come;
Your will be done
On earth as it is in heaven.

MATTHEW 6:9-10

TAKE A MOMENT TO AFFIRM THE TRUTH OF THESE WORDS FROM SCRIPTURE, AND ASK GOD TO MAKE THEM A GROWING REALITY IN YOUR LIFE.

The word of God is living and active and sharper than any double-edged sword, piercing even to the dividing of soul and spirit and of joints and marrow; and it judges the thoughts and attitudes of the heart. And there is no creature hidden from His sight, but everything is uncovered and laid bare before the eyes of Him to whom we must give account.

HEBREWS 4:12-13

The law was added that the transgression might increase. But where sin increased, grace abounded all the more so that just as sin reigned in death, so also grace might reign through righteousness to bring eternal life through Jesus Christ our Lord.

ROMANS 5:20-21

Lord, I thank You for Your penetrating and profound Word that illuminates my path and directs me in the truth. May I respond to Your gracious initiatives and walk in the way of eternal life.

PRAYING FOR BELIEVERS
Thanksgiving

O Lord, I am deeply grateful for Your
wonderful acts, for Your abundant promises,
and for the gift of my relationship with You
through the merits of Christ.

*All the kings of the earth will give thanks to You, O Lord,
when they hear the words of Your mouth. Yes, they sing of
the ways of the Lord, for the glory of the Lord is great.
Though the Lord is on high, yet He looks upon the lowly, but
the proud He knows from afar.*

PSALM 138:4-6

TAKE A MOMENT TO EXPRESS YOUR GRATI-
TUDE FOR THE MANY BLESSINGS THAT YOU
HAVE RECEIVED FROM THE LORD.

*We should always thank God
for other believers, mentioning them in our prayers.*

1 THESSALONIANS 1:2

We should always pray for other believers, that our God may count them worthy of His calling and fulfill every desire for goodness and every work of faith with power.

2 THESSALONIANS 1:11

Lord, I thank You for Your glorious works and for Christ, the Man from heaven. I thank You for the peace Jesus gives to me, and I ask that I would remember other believers in my prayers.

PERSEVERING UNDER TRIAL
Adoration

Lord, I give thanks for Your greatness, your goodness, and your love; and I now draw near to enjoy your presence.

> The word of the Lord is upright,
> And all His work is done in faithfulness.
> He loves righteousness and justice;
> The earth is full of the lovingkindness of the Lord.
>
> PSALM 33:4-5

Once God has spoken; twice I have heard this: that power belongs to God, and that You, O Lord, are loving. For You reward each person according to what he has done.

PSALM 62:11-12

TAKE A MOMENT TO CONSIDER GOD'S AWESOME MAJESTY, AND THANK HIM THAT HE LOVES YOU AND WANTS AN INTIMATE RELATIONSHIP WITH YOU.

I desire to be diligent to realize the full assurance of hope to the end. I do not want to become sluggish but to imitate those who through faith and patience inherit the promises.

HEBREWS 6:11-12

Blessed is the man who perseveres under trial because when he has been approved, he will receive the crown of life that God has promised to those who love Him.

JAMES 1:12

*L*ord, I thank You that You are my Redeemer. You gave me the gift of life. I thank You for making me Your child and heir. May I persevere under trials and receive the crown of life.

LEARNING GOD'S WAYS
Confession

I am grateful to You, *O God*, for the blessing of your forgiveness. I thank You that in Christ You set me free from the guilt of the past and give me hope for the future.

When I have sinned against You, hear from heaven and forgive my sin and restore me. Teach me the good way in which I should walk. When I sin against You—for there is no one who does not sin—may I return to You with all my heart and with all my soul.

1 KINGS 8:33-34, 36, 46, 48

TAKE A MOMENT TO ASK THE SPIRIT TO SEARCH YOUR HEART AND REVEAL ANY AREAS OF UNCONFESSED SIN. ACKNOWLEDGE THESE TO THE LORD, AND THANK HIM FOR HIS FORGIVENESS.

A hot-tempered man stirs up dissension,
but he who is slow to anger calms a quarrel.

PROVERBS 15:18

I will not mistreat my neighbor,
but I will fear my God; for You are the Lord my God.

LEVITICUS 25:17

*L*ord, I thank You that Christ has been given all authority and that His body and blood purchased my salvation. I thank You for my heavenly citizenship; and I ask that I would treat You with awe and respect, that I would be slow to anger.

AVOIDING SIN
Renewal

I praise You, $\mathcal{L}ord$, that You are intimately acquainted with my ways and that You always love me and have my best interests at heart.

> *Like Noah, may I be a righteous person,*
> *blameless among the people of my time,*
> *and one who walks with God.*
>
> GENESIS 6:9
>
> *Like Moses, may I do according to all*
> *that the Lord commands me.*
>
> EXODUS 39:42, 40:16

TAKE A MOMENT TO OFFER THIS DAY TO THE LORD, AND ASK HIM FOR THE GRACE TO GROW IN YOUR KNOWLEDGE AND LOVE FOR HIM.

In my anger I will not sin;
I will not let the sun go down while I am still angry,
and I will not give the devil a foothold.

EPHESIANS 4:26-27

Starting a quarrel is like breaching a dam,
so I will stop a quarrel before it breaks out.

PROVERBS 17:14

*L*ord, I praise You for Your sovereign power and thank You for Your promise of complete renewal. I thank You for the many things You have given me, and I ask that I would be self-controlled and live in peace with others.

OVERCOMING TO INHERIT
Petition

As I approach Your throne of grace today, I am grateful that You care about the things that concern me and that You want me to offer them up to You.

We are looking for the blessed hope and the glorious appearing of our great God and Savior, Christ Jesus, who gave Himself for us to redeem us from all iniquity and to purify for Himself a people for His own possession.

TITUS 2:13-14

TAKE A MOMENT TO SHARE YOUR PERSONAL NEEDS WITH GOD, INCLUDING YOUR PHYSICAL, EMOTIONAL, RELATIONAL, AND SPIRITUAL CONCERNS.

Ah, Lord God! You have made the heavens and the earth by Your great power and outstretched arm. Nothing is too difficult for You. You are the great and mighty God, whose name is the Lord of hosts. You are great in counsel and mighty in deed, and Your eyes are open to all the ways of the sons of men.

JEREMIAH 32:17-19

You are the Alpha and the Omega, the Beginning and the End. To the one who is thirsty, You will give to drink without cost from the spring of the water of life.

REVELATION 21:6

Lord, nothing is too difficult for You, the living God who spoke the cosmos into being and orders all things in Your providential care. May I live as one who overcomes the world and inherits Your blessed promises.

DOING ALL FOR GOD'S GLORY
Intercession

Lord, You have invited me to pray for the needs of others; and since You desire what is best for them, I take this opportunity to bring these requests to You.

Jesus said, "As the Father has sent Me, I also send you."

JOHN 20:21

Grant that I may be used to open the eyes of others and to turn them from darkness to light, and from the power of Satan to God so that they may receive forgiveness of sins and an inheritance among those who have been sanctified by faith in Jesus.

ACTS 26:18

TAKE A MOMENT TO LIFT UP THE NEEDS OF YOUR FAMILY AND FRIENDS, AND TO OFFER UP ANY OTHER BURDENS FOR OTHERS THAT THE LORD BRINGS TO MIND.

*I do not want to love praise from men
more than praise from God.*

JOHN 12:43

Whatever I do, I should do all to the glory of God.

1 CORINTHIANS 10:31

$\mathcal{L}ord$, I thank You that Jesus so clearly manifested Your perfection and that He will come again in power and glory. I thank You for Your provision in times of temptation, and I ask for the grace to seek Your praise rather than that of people.

ACKNOWLEDGING JESUS
Affirmation

God, I want Your Word to be deeply implanted in me so that I not only know the truth but also express it in the way I live.

May our Lord Jesus Christ Himself and God our Father, who has loved us and has given us eternal consolation and good hope by grace, comfort our hearts and strengthen us in every good work and word.

2 THESSALONIANS 2:16-17

TAKE A MOMENT TO AFFIRM THE TRUTH OF THESE WORDS FROM SCRIPTURE, AND ASK GOD TO MAKE THEM A GROWING REALITY IN YOUR LIFE.

Whoever acknowledges You before men, You will also acknowledge him before Your Father in heaven. But whoever denies You before men, You will also deny him before Your Father in heaven.

MATTHEW 10:32-33

I will not be ashamed to testify about our Lord, but I will join with others in suffering for the gospel according to the power of God.

2 TIMOTHY 1:8

Lord, I thank You that Your promises are sure and that You will create new heavens and a new earth. I thank You for choosing me to bear fruit, and I ask that I would acknowledge Jesus Christ before others.

USING MY MOUTH TO BLESS
Thanksgiving

O Lord, I am deeply grateful for Your wonderful acts, for Your abundant promises, and for the gift of my relationship with You through the merits of Christ.

Bless the Lord, O my soul;
And all that is within me, bless His holy name.
Bless the Lord, O my soul,
And forget not all His benefits;
Who forgives all your iniquities
And heals all your diseases;
Who redeems your life from the pit
And crowns you with love and compassion;
Who satisfies your desires with good things,
So that your youth is renewed like the eagle's.

PSALM 103:1-5

TAKE A MOMENT TO EXPRESS YOUR GRATITUDE FOR THE MANY BLESSINGS THAT YOU HAVE RECEIVED FROM THE LORD.

When pride comes, then comes dishonor,
but with humility comes wisdom.

PROVERBS 11:2

The tongue also is a fire, a world of evil that is set among the parts of the body, that corrupts the whole body, and sets the whole course of our life on fire and is set on fire by hell.

JAMES 3:6

Lord, thank You that You have given all things into Your Son's hand and that He has become the ladder to heaven. Thank You that I belong to Christ. Please guard me from pride and boasting.

GIVING IN GOOD MEASURE
Adoration

Lord, I give thanks for Your greatness, your goodness, and your love; and I now draw near to enjoy your presence.

A great multitude, which no one could number, from all nations and tribes and peoples and languages will stand before the throne and before the Lamb, clothed with white robes with palm branches in their hands, and will cry out with a loud voice, "Salvation belongs to our God, who sits on the throne, and to the Lamb!"

REVELATION 7:9-10

Blessed is the King who comes in the name of the Lord!

LUKE 19:38

TAKE A MOMENT TO CONSIDER GOD'S AWESOME MAJESTY, AND THANK HIM THAT HE LOVES YOU AND WANTS AN INTIMATE RELATIONSHIP WITH YOU.

Whoever gives another a cup of water to drink because of his name as a follower of Christ will by no means lose his reward.

MARK 9:41

When I give, it will be given to me; good measure, pressed down, shaken together, running over, will be poured into my lap.

LUKE 6:38

Lord, I praise You that You are the Alpha and the Omega. Thank You that Jesus had the authority and chose to lay down His life and to take it up again. Please deliver me from every evil work. May I be generous in my service to others.

SETTING MY HOPE IN JESUS
Confession

I am grateful to You, O God, for the blessing of your forgiveness. I thank You that in Christ You set me free from the guilt of the past and give me hope for the future.

I will endure discipline, for God is treating me as a son. For what son is not disciplined by his father? If I am without discipline, of which all have become partakers, then I am an illegitimate child and not a true son.

HEBREWS 12:7-8

TAKE A MOMENT TO ASK THE SPIRIT TO SEARCH YOUR HEART AND REVEAL ANY AREAS OF UNCONFESSED SIN. ACKNOWLEDGE THESE TO THE LORD, AND THANK HIM FOR HIS FORGIVENESS.

I will prepare my mind for action and be self-controlled, setting my hope fully on the grace to be brought to me at the revelation of Jesus Christ.

1 PETER 1:13

I will be self-controlled and alert; my adversary the devil prowls around like a roaring lion looking for someone to devour. But I will resist him, standing firm in the faith, knowing that my brothers throughout the world are undergoing the same kind of sufferings.

1 PETER 5:8-9

Lord, You are the source of all things and the resurrected Christ perfectly fulfilled the Scriptures. I thank You for Your deliverance. May I be self-controlled and firm in my faith.

FIGHTING THE GOOD FIGHT
Renewal

I praise You, *Lord*, that You are intimately acquainted with my ways and that You always love me and have my best interests at heart.

> *Christ must increase; I must decrease.*
>
> JOHN 3:30

You are the true vine, and Your Father is the vinedresser. May I abide in You, and You in me. As the branch cannot bear fruit of itself, unless it abides in the vine, neither can I, unless I abide in You.

JOHN 15:1,4

TAKE A MOMENT TO OFFER THIS DAY TO THE LORD, AND ASK HIM FOR THE GRACE TO GROW IN YOUR KNOWLEDGE AND LOVE FOR HIM.

I will fight the good fight of faith and lay hold of the eternal life to which I was called when I made the good confession in the presence of many witnesses.

1 TIMOTHY 6:12

I will not return evil for evil or insult for insult, but blessing instead, because to this I was called, that I may inherit a blessing.

1 PETER 3:9

Lord, I praise. You alone are God and I rejoice that the resurrected Christ is the firstfruits of those who will be raised from the dead. I thank You for the inheritance You have given to me, and I ask that I would remain faithful in the good fight of faith.

TRAINING UP A CHILD
Petition

As I approach Your throne of grace today, I am grateful that You care about the things that concern me and that You want me to offer them up to You.

> Let me hear Your unfailing love in the morning,
> For I have put my trust in You.
> Show me the way I should walk,
> For to You I lift up my soul.
>
> PSALM 143:8

TAKE A MOMENT TO SHARE YOUR PER-
SONAL NEEDS WITH GOD, INCLUDING
YOUR PHYSICAL, EMOTIONAL, RELATIONAL,
AND SPIRITUAL CONCERNS.

*I will train up each child according to his way;
even when he is old he will not depart from it.*

PROVERBS 22:6

*Correct your son, and he will give you rest;
he will bring delight to your soul.*

PROVERBS 29:17

*L*ord, I praise You that You are clothed with majesty, and thank You that Jesus came to set us free. I thank You for Your gift of eternal life through faith in Christ, and I ask that I would instruct others in the way of righteousness and truth.

LEARNING TO DO GOOD
Intercession

Lord, You have invited me to pray for the needs of others; and since You desire what is best for them, I take this opportunity to bring these requests to You.

May I help the weak and remember the words of the Lord Jesus, that He said, "It is more blessed to give than to receive."

ACTS 20:35

May I learn to do good,
Seek justice,
Remove the oppressor,
Defend the orphan,
And plead for the widow.

ISAIAH 1:17

TAKE A MOMENT TO LIFT UP THE NEEDS OF YOUR FAMILY AND FRIENDS, AND TO OFFER UP ANY OTHER BURDENS FOR OTHERS THAT THE LORD BRINGS TO MIND.

*How good and pleasant it is when
brothers live together in unity!*

PSALM 133:1

*May those who hope in You not be ashamed because of me,
O Lord God of hosts; may those who seek You not be
dishonored because of me, O God of Israel.*

PSALM 69:6

Lord, I praise You for Your majestic holiness and for Jesus, the good Shepherd. I thank You that I am a new creation in Christ, and I ask that people would honor You because of the way I live.

129

Affirmation

God, I want Your Word to be deeply implanted in me so that I not only know the truth but also express it in the way I live.

To the King eternal, immortal, invisible, the only God, be honor and glory forever and ever.

1 TIMOTHY 1:17

The God of all grace, who called me to His eternal glory in Christ, after I have suffered a little while, will Himself perfect, confirm, strengthen, and establish me. To him be the glory and dominion for ever and ever. Amen.

1 PETER 5:10-11

TAKE A MOMENT TO AFFIRM THE TRUTH OF THESE WORDS FROM SCRIPTURE, AND ASK GOD TO MAKE THEM A GROWING REALITY IN YOUR LIFE.

We have the prophetic word made more certain, to which I will do well to pay attention, as to a light shining in a dark place, until the day dawns and the morning star rises in my heart.

2 PETER 1:19

I will learn to fear You all the days I live on the earth and teach Your words to my children.

DEUTERONOMY 4:10

*L*ord, I thank You for searching and knowing me and for giving me rest in Christ. I thank You for the indwelling Comforter, and I ask that I would observe Your word and teach it to others.

Thanksgiving

O Lord, I am deeply grateful for Your wonderful acts, for Your abundant promises, and for the gift of my relationship with You through the merits of Christ.

> The Lord is close to the brokenhearted
> And saves those who are crushed in spirit.
> Many are the afflictions of the righteous,
> But the Lord delivers him out of them all.
>
> PSALM 34:18-19
>
> God is my refuge and strength,
> An ever-present help in trouble.
>
> PSALM 46:1

TAKE A MOMENT TO EXPRESS YOUR GRATITUDE FOR THE MANY BLESSINGS THAT YOU HAVE RECEIVED FROM THE LORD.

Whatever is true, whatever is noble, whatever is right, whatever is pure, whatever is lovely, whatever is of good report—if anything is excellent or praiseworthy—I will think about such things. The things I have learned and received and heard and seen in those who walk with Christ I will practice, and the God of peace will be with me.

PHILIPPIANS 4:8-9

There is neither Jew nor Greek, there is neither slave nor free, there is neither male nor female, for we are all one in Christ Jesus.

GALATIANS 3:28

Lord, praise You that Your righteousness endures forever and that Christ died for my sins once for all. I thank You for being my light and salvation. May I set my mind on those things please You.

SINGING HIS PRAISE
Adoration

Lord, I give thanks for Your greatness, your goodness, and your love; and I now draw near to enjoy your presence.

> The Lord Most High is awesome,
> The great King over all the earth!
> God is the King of all the earth,
> And I will sing His praise.
>
> PSALM 47:2, 7

> You must be treated as holy by those who come near You,
> and before all people, You will be honored.
>
> LEVITICUS 10:3

TAKE A MOMENT TO CONSIDER GOD'S AWESOME MAJESTY, AND THANK HIM THAT HE LOVES YOU AND WANTS AN INTIMATE RELATIONSHIP WITH YOU.

With the tongue we praise our Lord and Father, and with it we curse men, who have been made in the likeness of God; out of the same mouth come blessing and cursing, and this should not be.

JAMES 3:9-10

We should all be of one mind and be sympathetic, loving as brothers, compassionate, and humble.

1 PETER 3:8

$\mathscr{L}ord$, I praise You for Your majesty and for the saving work of Your Son. I thank You that I have confessed the Lord Jesus with my mouth, and I ask for the power to restrain my tongue and to be compassionate to others.

LIFTING UP HIS NAME
Confession

I am grateful to You, *O God*, for the blessing of your forgiveness. I thank You that in Christ You set me free from the guilt of the past and give me hope for the future.

O Lord, revive Your work in the midst of the years, In our time make them known; In wrath remember mercy.

HABAKKUK 3:2

If You, Lord, should mark iniquities,
O Lord, who could stand?
But there is forgiveness with You,
That You may be feared.

PSALM 130:3-4

TAKE A MOMENT TO ASK THE SPIRIT TO SEARCH YOUR HEART AND REVEAL ANY AREAS OF UNCONFESSED SIN. ACKNOW-LEDGE THESE TO THE LORD, AND THANK HIM FOR HIS FORGIVENESS.

The heavens will praise Your wonders, O Lord, Your faithfulness also in the assembly of the holy ones. For who in the heavens can be compared with the Lord? Who is like the Lord among the sons of the mighty?

PSALM 89:5-6

From the rising to the setting of the sun,
Your name will be great among the nations.

MALACHI 1:11

Lord, I praise You for Your matchless mercies and for Your loyal love. You are high and exalted above all. There is no one like You. You are the awesome God of faithfulness and love. May your name be great in my heart.

137

BEING RICH TOWARD GOD
Renewal

I praise You, *Lord*, that You are intimately acquainted with my ways and that You always love me and have my best interests at heart.

May I not turn aside from following the Lord, but serve the Lord with all my heart. May I not turn aside to go after worthless things which do not profit or deliver.

1 SAMUEL 12:20-21

The works of the flesh are evident, which are: immorality, impurity, sensuality, idolatry, sorcery, hatred, discord, jealousy, fits of rage, selfish ambition, dissensions, factions, envyings, drunkenness, revelries, and the like. . . . But the fruit of the Spirit is love, joy, peace, patience, kindness, goodness, faithfulness, gentleness, self-control; against such things there is no law.

GALATIANS 5:19-23

TAKE A MOMENT TO OFFER THIS DAY TO THE LORD, AND ASK HIM FOR THE GRACE TO GROW IN YOUR KNOWLEDGE AND LOVE FOR HIM.

I will not worry about tomorrow, for tomorrow will worry about itself. Each day has enough trouble of its own.

MATTHEW 6:34

I do not want to lay up treasure for myself without being rich toward God.

LUKE 12:21

$\mathcal{L}ord$, all things serve You. You and Your works are wonderful. I thank You that I can find comfort through hope in You. May I not worry about worldly things, but seek to be rich toward You.

PURSUING OTHERS' GOOD
Petition

As I approach Your throne of grace today, I am grateful that You care about the things that concern me and that You want me to offer them up to You.

May my conscience testify that I have conducted myself in the world in the holiness and sincerity that are from God, not in fleshly wisdom but in the grace of God, especially in my relations with others.

2 CORINTHIANS 1:12

TAKE A MOMENT TO SHARE YOUR PERSONAL NEEDS WITH GOD, INCLUDING YOUR PHYSICAL, EMOTIONAL, RELATIONAL, AND SPIRITUAL CONCERNS.

I will not repay evil for evil to anyone,
but I will pursue what is good for others.

1 THESSALONIANS 5:15

I will treat subordinates with respect, not threatening them,
knowing that both their Master and mine is in heaven; and
there is no partiality with Him.

EPHESIANS 6:9

Lord, I praise You that You are the ruler of all things and that You save the humble. I thank You for Your goodness, and I ask that I would pursue what is in the best interests of others.

WALKING THE WAY OF THE BLAMELESS
Intercession

Lord, You have invited me to pray for the needs of others; and since You desire what is best for them, I take this opportunity to bring these requests to You.

Salvation belongs to the Lord.
May Your blessing be on Your people.

PSALM 3:8

Let all who take refuge in You be glad;
Let them ever sing for joy,
Because You defend them.
And let those who love Your name be joyful in You.

PSALM 5:11

TAKE A MOMENT TO LIFT UP THE NEEDS OF YOUR FAMILY AND FRIENDS, AND TO OFFER UP ANY OTHER BURDENS FOR OTHERS THAT THE LORD BRINGS TO MIND.

The righteousness of the blameless makes a straight way for them, but the wicked will fall by their own wickedness.

PROVERBS 11:5

The path of the righteous is like the first gleam of dawn, shining ever brighter until the full light of day. But the way of the wicked is like darkness; they do not know what makes them stumble.

PROVERBS 4:18-19

Lord, I thank You that Jesus is the resurrection and the life and that every knee will bow before Him. I thank You for the gift of His righteousness, and I ask that I would walk in His power and light.

SINGING WITH GRATITUDE
Affirmation

God, I want Your Word to be deeply implanted in me so that I not only know the truth but also express it in the way I live.

May the God of peace, who through the blood of the eternal covenant brought back from the dead our Lord Jesus, that great Shepherd of the sheep, equip us in every good thing to do His will, working in us what is pleasing in His sight, through Jesus Christ, to whom be glory forever and ever.

HEBREWS 13:20-21

TAKE A MOMENT TO AFFIRM THE TRUTH OF THESE WORDS FROM SCRIPTURE, AND ASK GOD TO MAKE THEM A GROWING REALITY IN YOUR LIFE.

Reckless words pierce like a sword,
but the tongue of the wise brings healing.

PROVERBS 12:18

We should let the word of Christ dwell in us richly as we teach and admonish one another with all wisdom and as we sing psalms, hymns, and spiritual songs with gratitude in our hearts to God.

COLOSSIANS 3:16

Lord, I thank You that You are incomparable and that Your Son will come as the KING OF KINGS and LORD OF LORDS. I thank You for calling me to become like a little child, and I ask that my words would build others up and not tear them down.

LIVING IN ANTICIPATION
Thanksgiving

O Lord, I am deeply grateful for Your wonderful acts, for Your abundant promises, and for the gift of my relationship with You through the merits of Christ.

We give thanks to You, O God, we give thanks,
For Your name is near.

PSALM 75:1

Truth shall spring forth from the earth,
And righteousness looks down from heaven.

PSALM 85:11

TAKE A MOMENT TO EXPRESS YOUR GRATITUDE FOR THE MANY BLESSINGS THAT YOU HAVE RECEIVED FROM THE LORD.

I will give thanks to the Lord, for He is good; His lovingkindness endures forever. I will give thanks to the Lord for His unfailing love and His wonderful acts to the children of men, for He satisfies the thirsty soul and fills the hungry soul with good things.

PSALM 107:1, 8-9

When the Son of Man comes in His glory, and all the angels with Him, He will sit on His glorious throne. Then the King will say to those on His right, "Come, you who are blessed by My Father; inherit the kingdom prepared for you since the foundation of the world."

MATTHEW 25:31, 34

Lord, Your promises are sure, Your love is unceasing, and Your kindness is boundless. May I live in holy anticipation of the coming of the Lord Jesus and His glorious kingdom.

ASCRIBING GLORY TO GOD
Adoration

Lord, I give thanks for Your greatness, your goodness, and your love; and I now draw near to enjoy your presence.

The Lord is great and greatly to be praised; He is to be feared above all gods. For all the gods of the nations are idols, but the Lord made the heavens. Splendor and majesty are before Him; strength and joy are in His place. I will ascribe to the Lord glory and strength. I will ascribe to the Lord the glory due His name and worship the Lord in the beauty of holiness. Tremble before him, all the earth. The world is firmly established, it will not be moved.

1 CHRONICLES 16:25-30

You are the God of Abraham and the Fear of Isaac.

GENESIS 31:42

TAKE A MOMENT TO CONSIDER GOD'S AWESOME MAJESTY, AND THANK HIM THAT HE LOVES YOU AND WANTS AN INTIMATE RELATIONSHIP WITH YOU.

Teach me to number my days,
that I may gain a heart of wisdom.

PSALM 90:12

The fear of the Lord, that is wisdom,
and to depart from evil is understanding.

JOB 28:28

*L*ord, You are the Lord of the heavens and the earth. I thank You for Your mercy and faithfulness. May I recognize the brevity of my earthly sojourn and live in wisdom.

BEING A PERSON OF FAITH
Confession

I am grateful to You, O God, for the blessing of your forgiveness. I thank You that in Christ You set me free from the guilt of the past and give me hope for the future.

Save me from bloodguilt, O God,
The God of my salvation,
And my tongue will sing aloud of Your righteousness.
For You do not desire sacrifice, or I would bring it;
You do not delight in burnt offering.
The sacrifices of God are a broken spirit;
A broken and contrite heart,
O God, You will not despise.

PSALM 51:14, 16-17

TAKE A MOMENT TO ASK THE SPIRIT TO SEARCH YOUR HEART AND REVEAL ANY AREAS OF UNCONFESSED SIN. ACKNOWLEDGE THESE TO THE LORD, AND THANK HIM FOR HIS FORGIVENESS.

*Like Ezra, I want to set my heart to study the word
of the Lord, and to do it, and to teach it to others.*

Ezra 7:10

*I want to be a person of faith, who does not doubt the
promises of God, and not a double-minded man, who is
unstable in all his ways.*

James 1:6, 8

*Lord, I praise You for Your wisdom and
strength and for Your authority over all
things. I thank You for the assurance of the
resurrection. May I know Your Word and
hope in Your promises.*

LOVING MY ENEMIES
Renewal

I praise You, *Lord*, that You are intimately acquainted with my ways and that You always love me and have my best interests at heart.

May I remove the places of idolatry from my life, and like Asa, let my heart be fully committed to God all my days.

2 CHRONICLES 15:17

May I trust in the Lord and do good; may I dwell in the land and feed on Your faithfulness. When I delight myself in the Lord, You will give me the desires of my heart. I will commit my way to the Lord and trust in You, and You will bring it to pass.

PSALM 37:3-5

TAKE A MOMENT TO OFFER THIS DAY TO THE LORD, AND ASK HIM FOR THE GRACE TO GROW IN YOUR KNOWLEDGE AND LOVE FOR HIM.

I will love my enemies, do good to them. . . .
for He is kind to the ungrateful and evil.

LUKE 6:35

I will bear with others and forgive whatever
complaints I have against them;
I will forgive just as the Lord forgave me.

COLOSSIANS 3:13

Lord, I praise You for Your righteous and glorious throne. You created me in Christ Jesus for good works. May I be merciful and love those who do not love me. May I demonstrate forbearance and forgiveness.

PUTTING ON THE LORD JESUS CHRIST

Petition

As I approach Your throne of grace today, I am grateful that You care about the things that concern me and that You want me to offer them up to You.

May I learn to be content in whatever circumstances I am. Whether I am abased or in abundance, whether I am filled or hungry, let me learn the secret of being content in any and every situation. I can do all things through Him who strengthens me.

PHILIPPIANS 4:11-13

TAKE A MOMENT TO SHARE YOUR PERSONAL NEEDS WITH GOD, INCLUDING YOUR PHYSICAL, EMOTIONAL, RELATIONAL, AND SPIRITUAL CONCERNS.

The thoughts of the righteous are just,
but the advice of the wicked is deceitful.

PROVERBS 12:5

I will walk properly as in the daytime, not in revellings and drunkenness, not in promiscuity and debauchery, not in strife and jealousy. Rather, I will put on the Lord Jesus Christ and make no provision to gratify the lusts of the flesh.

ROMANS 13:13-14

Lord, I thank You for Your perfect precepts and commandments and for the gift of Your indwelling Holy Spirit. I thank You that You are my high tower and my deliverer, and I ask that my thoughts and actions would honor the Lord Jesus Christ.

ℐHOLDING FAST TO WHAT IS GOOD
Intercession

ℒ*ord, You have invited me to pray for the needs of others; and since You desire what is best for them, I take this opportunity to bring these requests to You.*

For the commandments, "You shall not commit adultery," "You shall not murder," "You shall not steal," "You shall not covet," and if there is any other commandment, it is summed up in this saying: "You shall love your neighbor as yourself."

ROMANS 13:9

TAKE A MOMENT TO LIFT UP THE NEEDS OF YOUR FAMILY AND FRIENDS, AND TO OFFER UP ANY OTHER BURDENS FOR OTHERS THAT THE LORD BRINGS TO MIND.

The wisdom that comes from above is first pure, then peaceable, gentle, submissive, full of mercy and good fruits, without partiality and hypocrisy. And the fruit of righteousness is sown in peace by those who make peace.

JAMES 3:17-18

I will examine all things, hold fast to the good, and abstain from every form of evil.

1 THESSALONIANS 5:21-22

Lord, I praise You for Your magnificent work in creation and thank You for making the light of the knowledge of Christ shine in my heart. May I practice the wisdom that comes from above and cling to the good, avoiding every form of evil.

Affirmation

God, I want Your Word to be deeply implanted in me so that I not only know the truth but also express it in the way I live.

You are worthy, our Lord and God,
To receive glory and honor and power,
For You created all things,
And by Your will they were created and have their being.

REVELATION 4:11

Blessed is the man who listens to wisdom, watching daily at her gates, waiting at her doorposts. For whoever finds wisdom finds life and obtains favor from the Lord.

PROVERBS 8:34-35

TAKE A MOMENT TO AFFIRM THE TRUTH OF THESE WORDS FROM SCRIPTURE, AND ASK GOD TO MAKE THEM A GROWING REALITY IN YOUR LIFE.

I will receive the words of wisdom and treasure her commands within me. If I cry for discernment and lift up my voice for understanding, if I seek her as silver and search for her as for hidden treasures, then I will understand the fear of the Lord and find the knowledge of God.

PROVERBS 2:1, 3-5

Lord, I praise You for Your sovereign majesty and for the heavens that proclaim the work of Your hands. I ask that I would rejoice and be thankful in all things and that I would listen to wisdom and apply my heart to understanding.

Thanksgiving

O Lord, I am deeply grateful for Your wonderful acts, for Your abundant promises, and for the gift of my relationship with You through the merits of Christ.

This poor man cried out, and the Lord heard him, and saved him out of all his troubles. The angel of the Lord encamps around those who fear Him, and delivers them.

PSALM 34:6-7

I waited patiently for the Lord, and He turned to me and heard my cry. God lifted me out of the slimy pit, out of the mud and mire; He set my feet on a rock and gave me a firm place to stand. He put a new song in my mouth, a hymn of praise to our God. Many will see and fear and put their trust in the Lord.

PSALM 40:1-3

TAKE A MOMENT TO EXPRESS YOUR GRATITUDE FOR THE MANY BLESSINGS THAT YOU HAVE RECEIVED FROM THE LORD.

Whoever is wise and understanding will show it by his good conduct and works done in the humility that comes from wisdom.

JAMES 3:13

*I will commit my works to the Lord,
and my plans will be established.*

PROVERBS 16:3

Lord, I praise You. The Lord Jesus holds the key of David and He serves those in need. May I present my works to the Lord and be wise in heart, listening to counsel.

WRITING LOVE ON MY HEART
Adoration

Lord, I give thanks for Your greatness, your goodness, and your love; and I now draw near to enjoy your presence.

The Lord my God is God of gods and Lord of lords, the great God, mighty and awesome, who shows no partiality and accepts no bribes. He executes justice for the fatherless and the widow and loves the alien, giving him food and clothing.

DEUTERONOMY 10:17-18

My soul magnifies the Lord and my spirit rejoices in God my Savior, for the Mighty One has done great things for me, and holy is His name. His mercy is on those who fear Him, from generation to generation.

LUKE 1:46-47, 49-50

TAKE A MOMENT TO CONSIDER GOD'S AWESOME MAJESTY, AND THANK HIM THAT HE LOVES YOU AND WANTS AN INTIMATE RELATIONSHIP WITH YOU.

Blessed are the merciful, for they shall obtain mercy.

MATTHEW 5:7

I will not let love and truth leave me; I will bind them around my neck and write them on the tablet of my heart.

PROVERBS 3:3

Lord, I thank You for the justice and perfection of Your work and for Your promise of future glory. I thank You for gathering all things together in Christ, and I ask that I would be merciful, loving, and truthful.

*C*FISHING WITH JESUS
Confession

*I am grateful to You, O God, for the
blessing of your forgiveness. I thank You that
in Christ You set me free from the guilt of
the past and give me hope for the future.*

*God's eyes are on the ways of a person,
And He sees all their steps.
There is no darkness or deep shadow
Where the workers of iniquity can hide.
He does not need to examine a person further,
That they should go before God in judgment.*

JOB 34:21-23

TAKE A MOMENT TO ASK THE SPIRIT TO
SEARCH YOUR HEART AND REVEAL ANY
AREAS OF UNCONFESSED SIN. ACKNOW-
LEDGE THESE TO THE LORD, AND THANK
HIM FOR HIS FORGIVENESS.

I will not seek my own interests, but those of Christ Jesus.

PHILIPPIANS 2:21

As I follow You, You will make me a fisher of men.

MATTHEW 4:19, MARK 1:17

Lord, I praise You. All the treasures of wisdom and knowledge are hidden in Christ and He will return to the earth with power and great glory. I thank You for Your power and for Your precious promises, and I ask that I would seek the interests of Christ Jesus and share His life with others.

AVOIDING PRESUMPTION
Renewal

I praise You, *Lord*, that You are intimately acquainted with my ways and that You always love me and have my best interests at heart.

O Lord my God, may I fear You, walk in all Your ways,
love You, and serve You
with all my heart and with all my soul.

DEUTERONOMY 10:12

I have not been made perfect, but I press on to lay hold
of that for which Christ Jesus also laid hold of me.

PHILIPPIANS 3:12

TAKE A MOMENT TO OFFER THIS DAY TO THE LORD, AND ASK HIM FOR THE GRACE TO GROW IN YOUR KNOWLEDGE AND LOVE FOR HIM.

Instruct a wise person, and they will be wiser still; teach a righteous person, and they will increase in learning.

PROVERBS 9:9

I should not say, "Today or tomorrow I will go to this or that city, spend a year there, carry on business, and make a profit." For I do not even know what my life will be tomorrow. I am a vapor that appears for a little while and then vanishes away. . . . all such boasting is evil.

JAMES 4:13-16

Lord, You rule in sovereign majesty and Your Son has authority to give eternal life. May I put my hope in Your unfailing love, and grow in wisdom, avoiding presumption.

WALKING WISELY
Petition

As I approach Your throne of grace today, I am grateful that You care about the things that concern me and that You want me to offer them up to You.

Oh, that You would bless me and enlarge my territory! Let Your hand be with me and keep me from evil, so it may not grieve me.

1 CHRONICLES 4:10

Please regard Your servant's prayer and his supplication, O Lord my God. Listen to the cry and the prayer that Your servant is praying before You this day.

1 KINGS 8:28

TAKE A MOMENT TO SHARE YOUR PERSONAL NEEDS WITH GOD, INCLUDING YOUR PHYSICAL, EMOTIONAL, RELATIONAL, AND SPIRITUAL CONCERNS.

The wise in heart accept commands,
but a chattering fool will be thrown down.

PROVERBS 10:8

The way of a fool is right in his own eyes,
but a wise man listens to counsel.

PROVERBS 12:15

Lord, I praise You that You are the exalted Rock of my salvation. Thank You that the blood of Christ cleanses me from all impurity. I thank You for the light of Your presence, and I ask that I would be wise in heart and listen to counsel.

PROCLAIMING THE KINGDOM
Intercession

Lord, You have invited me to pray for the needs of others; and since You desire what is best for them, I take this opportunity to bring these requests to You.

Lord, there is no one besides You to help the powerless against the mighty. Help us, O Lord our God, for we rest in You. O Lord, You are our God; do not let humans prevail against You.

2 CHRONICLES 14:11

TAKE A MOMENT TO LIFT UP THE NEEDS OF YOUR FAMILY AND FRIENDS, AND TO OFFER UP ANY OTHER BURDENS FOR OTHERS THAT THE LORD BRINGS TO MIND.

As the Father sent the Son into the world, He also has sent us into the world. And He has prayed for those who will believe in Him through our message.

JOHN 17:18, 20

You have called me to go and proclaim the kingdom of God.

LUKE 9:60

Lord, I praise You that Your counsel will stand and that Your dominion extends to the ends of the earth. I thank You for Your wonderful works, and I ask for the power to proclaim Your kingdom.

STANDING HOLY AND BLAMELESS
Affirmation

God, I want Your Word to be deeply implanted in me so that I not only know the truth but also express it in the way I live.

Worthy is the Lamb, who was slain,
To receive power and riches and wisdom
And strength and honor and glory and blessing!

REVELATION 5:12

TAKE A MOMENT TO AFFIRM THE TRUTH OF THESE WORDS FROM SCRIPTURE, AND ASK GOD TO MAKE THEM A GROWING REALITY IN YOUR LIFE.

I want the Lord to establish my heart as blameless and holy before our God and Father at the coming of our Lord Jesus with all His saints.

1 THESSALONIANS 3:13

In my faith in our glorious Lord Jesus Christ, I will not show partiality to some people above others.

JAMES 2:1

Lord, I praise You for Your awesome dominion. Thank You for creating us, a people for Your own possession. I thank You for leading me in Christ's triumph, and I ask that You would establish my heart as blameless and holy before You.

MAKING PEACE
Thanksgiving

O Lord, I am deeply grateful for Your wonderful acts, for Your abundant promises, and for the gift of my relationship with You through the merits of Christ.

In Your unfailing love You have led the people You have redeemed. In Your strength You have guided them to Your holy dwelling. You brought them in and planted them in the mountain of Your inheritance—the place, O Lord, You made for Your dwelling; the sanctuary, O Lord, Your hands have established.

EXODUS 15:13, 17

TAKE A MOMENT TO EXPRESS YOUR GRATITUDE FOR THE MANY BLESSINGS THAT YOU HAVE RECEIVED FROM THE LORD.

You are the Lord our God, who brought Your people out of Egypt so that they would no longer be their slaves; You broke the bars of their yoke and enabled them to walk with heads held high.

LEVITICUS 26:13

*Better a little with the fear of the Lord
than great wealth with turmoil.*

PROVERBS 15:16

*I will not give cause for offense in anything
so that my ministry will not be discredited.*

2 CORINTHIANS 6:3

Lord, I praise You for Your creation and for Your authority over the heavens and the earth. I thank You for the hope of righteousness through Your Spirit, and I ask that my faith in Christ would make me a peacemaker.

LAYING UP TRUE TREASURE

Adoration

Lord, I give thanks for Your greatness, your goodness, and your love; and I now draw near to enjoy your presence.

Oh, the depth of the riches both of the wisdom and knowledge of God! How unsearchable are Your judgments, and Your ways past finding out! For who has known the mind of the Lord? Or who has been Your counselor? Or who has first given to You, that You should repay him? For from You and through You and to You are all things.

ROMANS 11:33-36

TAKE A MOMENT TO CONSIDER GOD'S AWESOME MAJESTY, AND THANK HIM THAT HE LOVES YOU AND WANTS AN INTIMATE RELATIONSHIP WITH YOU.

*Hallelujah! Salvation and glory and power belong to our
God, because His judgments are true and righteous.*

REVELATION 19:1-2

*I will lay up for myself treasures in heaven, where moth and
rust do not destroy and where thieves do not break in and
steal. For where my treasure is, there my heart will be also.*

MATTHEW 6:20-21, LUKE 12:34

*He who is generous will be blessed,
for he shares his food with the poor.*

PROVERBS 22:9

*Lord, I praise You for Your love and
faithfulness. Even Jesus came in humility as
a servant. Soon I will be resurrected by my
Redeemer. May I lay up spiritual treasures
by being generous to others.*

WALKING IN HUMILITY
Confession

I am grateful to You, O God, for the blessing of your forgiveness. I thank You that in Christ You set me free from the guilt of the past and give me hope for the future.

He will not turn His face from you if you return to Him.

2 CHRONICLES 30:9

Blessed is he whose transgression is forgiven, whose sin is covered. Blessed is the man to whom the Lord does not impute iniquity and in whose spirit is no deceit. I said, "I will confess my transgressions to the Lord," and You forgave the guilt of my sin.

PSALM 32:1-2, 5

TAKE A MOMENT TO ASK THE SPIRIT TO SEARCH YOUR HEART AND REVEAL ANY AREAS OF UNCONFESSED SIN. ACKNOWLEDGE THESE TO THE LORD, AND THANK HIM FOR HIS FORGIVENESS.

The Christian in humble circumstances should glory in their high position, and the one who is rich should glory in their humiliation, because they will pass away like a flower of the field.

JAMES 1:9-10

Better a meal of vegetables where there is love than a fattened calf with hatred.

PROVERBS 15:17

$\mathcal{L}$*ord,* I praise You for Your unrivaled splendor. Thank You for calling me to be a child of the light. I thank You for the power of Christ in me. May I walk in humility and love.

SPEAKING THE TRUTH
Renewal

I praise You, *Lord*, that You are intimately acquainted with my ways and that You always love me and have my best interests at heart.

Like Josiah, may I do what is right in the sight of the Lord, walking in the ways of David and not turning aside to the right or to the left.

2 CHRONICLES 34:1-2

Like Josiah, give me a tender and responsive heart so that I will humble myself before You when I hear Your word.

2 CHRONICLES 34:27

TAKE A MOMENT TO OFFER THIS DAY TO THE LORD, AND ASK HIM FOR THE GRACE TO GROW IN YOUR KNOWLEDGE AND LOVE FOR HIM.

May I walk in the steps of Jesus,
who often withdrew to lonely places and prayed.

MARK 1:35; LUKE 5:16

I will put away perversity from my mouth
and keep corrupt talk far from my lips.

PROVERBS 4:24

Each of us must put off falsehood and speak truthfully
to their neighbor, for we are members of one another.

EPHESIANS 4:25

*L*ord, I thank You for Your Son Jesus and for His earthly ministry. I thank You for being worthy of my complete trust, and I ask that my speech would not be corrupt but truthful.

Petition

As I approach Your throne of grace today, I am grateful that You care about the things that concern me and that You want me to offer them up to You.

May I discipline myself to godliness. For physical exercise profits a little, but godliness is profitable for all things, since it holds promise for both the present life and the life to come.

1 TIMOTHY 4:7-8

TAKE A MOMENT TO SHARE YOUR PERSONAL NEEDS WITH GOD, INCLUDING YOUR PHYSICAL, EMOTIONAL, RELATIONAL, AND SPIRITUAL CONCERNS.

If I lack wisdom, I should ask of God,
who gives generously to all without reproach,
and it will be given to me.

JAMES 1:5

I will watch carefully how I walk, not as the unwise but as wise, making the most of every opportunity, because the days are evil. I will not be foolish, but understand what the will of the Lord is.

EPHESIANS 5:15-17

$\mathcal{L}ord$, I thank You that You are my strength and my song and that in Christ Jesus, You have given me a new heart. I thank You for filling me with Your Holy Spirit, and I ask that You guide my steps according to Your wisdom.

TRUSTING IN HIM
Intercession

Lord, You have invited me to pray for the needs of others; and since You desire what is best for them, I take this opportunity to bring these requests to You.

The Spirit helps me in my weakness, for I do not know what I ought to pray for, but the Spirit Himself intercedes for me with groans that words cannot express. And He who searches the hearts knows the mind of the Spirit, because the Spirit intercedes for the saints according to the will of God.

ROMANS 8:26-27

TAKE A MOMENT TO LIFT UP THE NEEDS OF YOUR FAMILY AND FRIENDS, AND TO OFFER UP ANY OTHER BURDENS FOR OTHERS THAT THE LORD BRINGS TO MIND.

Cursed is the one who trusts in man, who depends on flesh for his strength and whose heart turns away from the Lord. But blessed is the man who trusts in the Lord, whose confidence is in Him.

JEREMIAH 17:5, 7

The fear of man brings a snare,
but he who trusts in the Lord is set on high.

PROVERBS 29:25

Lord, praise You for the greatness of Your mercies and for rescuing the life of the needy. Thank You that I am in Christ and Christ is in me. May I trust in You and not put my hope in people.

SILENCING THE IGNORANT
Affirmation

God, I want Your Word to be deeply implanted in me so that I not only know the truth but also express it in the way I live.

Every creature in heaven and on earth and under the earth
And on the sea and all that is in them, will sing:
"To Him who sits on the throne and to the Lamb
Be blessing and honor and glory and power
For ever and ever!"

REVELATION 5:13

TAKE A MOMENT TO AFFIRM THE TRUTH OF THESE WORDS FROM SCRIPTURE, AND ASK GOD TO MAKE THEM A GROWING REALITY IN YOUR LIFE.

*He who gets wisdom loves his own soul;
he who keeps understanding will find good.*

PROVERBS 19:8

I will submit myself for the Lord's sake to every human authority, whether to a king as being supreme, or to governors as sent by him to punish evildoers and to praise those who do right; for it is the will of God that by doing good I may silence the ignorance of foolish people.

1 PETER 2:13-15

Lord, I praise You for Your universal kingdom and for Your sovereignty over nature. I thank You for Jesus, the Savior of my soul, and I ask that I would have the wisdom to acknowledge Your designated spheres of authority.

REVERING THE MOST HIGH
Thanksgiving

O Lord, I am deeply grateful for Your wonderful acts, for Your abundant promises, and for the gift of my relationship with You through the merits of Christ.

> You have loved me with an everlasting love;
> You have drawn me with lovingkindness.
>
> JEREMIAH 31:3

> I will sing to the Lord, for He is highly exalted.
> The Lord is my strength and my song;
> He has become my salvation.
> He is my God, and I will praise Him,
> My father's God, and I will exalt Him.
>
> EXODUS 15:1-2

TAKE A MOMENT TO EXPRESS YOUR GRATITUDE FOR THE MANY BLESSINGS THAT YOU HAVE RECEIVED FROM THE LORD.

I will not fear those who kill the body but cannot kill the soul, but rather, I will fear the One who is able to destroy both soul and body in hell.

MATTHEW 10:28

I want to be more concerned about the things of God than the things of men.

MARK 8:33

Lord, I praise You for Your unblemished holiness. Thank You for Your promise to perfect those who revere Your name. I know the Spirit of the living God resides in my heart, and I ask that I would revere You more than human interests.

Adoration

Lord, I give thanks for Your greatness, your goodness, and your love; and I now draw near to enjoy your presence.

> The Lord . . . suspends the earth on nothing.
>
> JOB 26:7

> He who made the Pleiades and Orion
> And turns deep darkness into morning
> And darkens day into night,
> Who calls for the waters of the sea
> And pours them out over the face of the earth—
> The Lord is His name.
>
> AMOS 5:8

TAKE A MOMENT TO CONSIDER GOD'S AWESOME MAJESTY, AND THANK HIM THAT HE LOVES YOU AND WANTS AN INTIMATE RELATIONSHIP WITH YOU.

As one who has believed in God, I want to be careful to devote myself to doing what is good.

TITUS 3:8

In this is love, not that we loved God, but that He loved us and sent His Son to be the propitiation for our sins. Since God so loved us, we also ought to love one another. No one has ever seen God; but if we love one another, God abides in us, and His love is perfected in us.

1 JOHN 4:10-12

Lord, You are the source of all wisdom and You delivered me from the slavery of death. I thank You that Christ is the door of salvation. May I devote myself to doing good and to loving others.

WALKING IN THE LIGHT
Confession

I am grateful to You, O God, for the
blessing of your forgiveness. I thank You that
in Christ You set me free from the guilt of
the past and give me hope for the future.

Heal my soul, for I have sinned against You.

PSALM 41:4

The Lord guides the humble in what is right
And teaches the humble His way.

PSALM 25:9

TAKE A MOMENT TO ASK THE SPIRIT TO
SEARCH YOUR HEART AND REVEAL ANY
AREAS OF UNCONFESSED SIN. ACKNOW-
LEDGE THESE TO THE LORD, AND THANK
HIM FOR HIS FORGIVENESS.

I will walk as a child of light (for the fruit of the light consists in all goodness and righteousness and truth), learning what is pleasing to the Lord.

EPHESIANS 5:8-10

As He who called me is holy, so may I be holy in all my conduct because it is written: "You shall be holy, for I am holy."

1 PETER 1:15-16

Lord, there is no one like You. Thank You that You sent Jesus into the world so that we could enter into a relationship with You. Thank You for setting me free from the burden of my sins. May I walk as a child of light and conduct my affairs in holiness and sincerity.

GIVING CHEERFULLY
Renewal

I praise You, *Lord*, that You are intimately acquainted with my ways and that You always love me and have my best interests at heart.

May the name of the Lord Jesus be magnified in my life.

ACTS 19:17

In view of God's mercy, may I present my body as a living sacrifice, holy and pleasing to God, which is my reasonable service.

ROMANS 12:1

TAKE A MOMENT TO OFFER THIS DAY TO THE LORD, AND ASK HIM FOR THE GRACE TO GROW IN YOUR KNOWLEDGE AND LOVE FOR HIM.

I will give generously to others without a grudging heart.

DEUTERONOMY 15:10

He who sows sparingly will also reap sparingly, and he who sows bountifully will also reap bountifully. Each one should give as he has decided in his heart, not reluctantly or under compulsion; for God loves a cheerful giver. And God is able to make all grace abound to us so that, always having all sufficiency in everything, we may abound in every good work.

2 CORINTHIANS 9:6-8

Lord, I thank You for Your mercies and faithfulness. Your name is great. I thank You for the washing of regeneration and renewal by the Holy Spirit. May I sow bountifully by being generous to others.

BOWING BEFORE HIM
Petition

As I approach Your throne of grace today, I am grateful that You care about the things that concern me and that You want me to offer them up to You.

I do not have a high priest who is unable to sympathize with my weaknesses, but one who has been tempted in every way, just as I am, yet without sin. Therefore, I will approach the throne of grace with confidence so that I may receive mercy and find grace to help in time of need.

HEBREWS 4:15-16

TAKE A MOMENT TO SHARE YOUR PER-SONAL NEEDS WITH GOD, INCLUDING YOUR PHYSICAL, EMOTIONAL, RELATIONAL, AND SPIRITUAL CONCERNS.

The Lord is gracious and compassionate, slow to anger, and great in lovingkindness. The Lord is good to all, and His tender mercies are over all His works.

PSALM 145:8-9

It is written, "As I live, says the Lord, every knee will bow before Me, and every tongue will confess to God." So then, each of us will give an account of himself to God.

ROMANS 14:11-12

*L*ord, I thank You that You are indeed good to all who call upon Your name and who look to You as their refuge and hope. May I order my steps in my earthly sojourn as one who will appear before You.

*R*ULING MY SPIRIT
Intercession

*L*ord, You have invited me to pray for the needs of others; and since You desire what is best for them, I take this opportunity to bring these requests to You.

If I speak in the tongues of men and of angels, but have not love, I am only a resounding gong or a clanging cymbal. And if I have the gift of prophecy and understand all mysteries and all knowledge, and if I have all faith so as to remove mountains, but have not love, I am nothing. And if I give all my possessions to the poor, and if I deliver my body to be burned, but have not love, it profits me nothing.

1 CORINTHIANS 13:1-3

TAKE A MOMENT TO LIFT UP THE NEEDS OF YOUR FAMILY AND FRIENDS, AND TO OFFER UP ANY OTHER BURDENS FOR OTHERS THAT THE LORD BRINGS TO MIND.

*I will watch and pray so that
I will not fall into temptation.*

MATTHEW 26:41

*He who is slow to anger is better than the mighty,
and he who rules his spirit than he who takes a city.*

PROVERBS 16:32

*L*ord, I thank You that I have received grace from Jesus Christ's fullness. Nothing can separate me from the love of Christ. May I control my spirit and not fall into temptation.

CONSIDERING HIS LOVE

Affirmation

God, I want Your Word to be deeply implanted in me so that I not only know the truth but also express it in the way I live.

You are my hiding place and my shield;
I have put my hope in Your word.

PSALM 119:114

My help is in the name of the Lord,
Who made heaven and earth.

PSALM 124:8

TAKE A MOMENT TO AFFIRM THE TRUTH OF THESE WORDS FROM SCRIPTURE, AND ASK GOD TO MAKE THEM A GROWING REALITY IN YOUR LIFE.

There is a time for everything,
and a season for every activity under heaven.

ECCLESIASTES 3:1

Whoever is wise will consider the lovingkindness
of the Lord.

PSALM 107:43

*L*ord, I praise You that You are everlasting. I thank You that You promise to raise me from the dead so that I can live with You forever. I pray that I will be a faithful steward of Your possessions, and I ask that I would walk in wisdom by doing the right thing at the right time in the right way.

Thanksgiving

O Lord, I am deeply grateful for Your wonderful acts, for Your abundant promises, and for the gift of my relationship with You through the merits of Christ.

> *Because I love You, You will deliver me;*
> *You will protect me, for I acknowledge Your name.*
> *I will call upon You, and You will answer me;*
> *You will be with me in trouble,*
> *You will deliver me and honor me.*
> *With long life You will satisfy me*
> *And show me Your salvation.*
>
> PSALM 91:14-16

TAKE A MOMENT TO EXPRESS YOUR GRATITUDE FOR THE MANY BLESSINGS THAT YOU HAVE RECEIVED FROM THE LORD.

*I will discipline my child while there is hope
and not be a willing party to his death.*

PROVERBS 19:18

*The rod and reproof impart wisdom,
but a child left to himself brings shame to his mother.*

PROVERBS 29:15

*L*ord, I thank You that You are my shield
and a refuge and that You save the humble.
I thank You that Jesus came as the One
who served, and I ask that I would serve
others by imparting Your truth to them.

People for Whom I am Praying

Answers to my Prayers

Keys to Using

A Simple Book of Prayers Effectively

- It is important that you do not merely read the words. Pray them in. Incorporate them into your own thoughts and experience.

- The opening words prepare you to draw near to God, followed by prayers adapted from Scripture. You may want to read these scripture prayers more than once. The prompt that follows the prayers invites you to pause and add your own thoughts and prayers.

- Each prayer concludes with a personal response to God concerning His person and works or with a prayer about your character or your relationships. After reflecting on these passages, use the closing prayer.

- Consider making a journal to add your own thoughts and prayers as they come to mind when using this book. You can also use this journal to record a list of prayers for yourself and for others as well as specific answers to prayer. We have added a few pages in the back for you to list the loved ones you pray for and the answers.

- To assist you in personalizing these prayers and affirmations, we have put them in the singular whenever possible. When you use *The Simple Book of Prayer* with another person or with a group, turn the singulars into plurals.

About the Authors

Kenneth Boa is author of
*Faith Has Its Reasons, Talk Thru the
Bible, Face to Face, Conformed to His
Image,* and many other books on
spiritual formation and apologetics.
He is a contributor to many study
Bibles, including *The Leadership Bible*
and the NASB *Zondervan Study
Bible.* He holds doctoral degrees
from New York University and
Oxford University in England.

Karen Boa has a B.A. from Montclair State University in
English and has done graduate work at New York University in
comparative literature. She continues to develop her interests in
literature, film, music and art, and is an avid gardener.

Additional copies of this book and other
titles by Kenneth and Karen Boa are
available from your local bookstore.

Also Available:
Seasons of Prayer
20 Compelling Evidences That God Exists
Simple Prayers for Women
Simple Prayers for Graduates

Please contact us at:

Honor Books
An Imprint of Cook Communication Ministries
4050 Lee Vance View
Colorado Springs, CO 89018

www.cookministries.com